AQUATIC ANIMAL QUARANTINE AND HEALTH CERTIFICATION IN ASIA

AQUATIC ANIMAL QUARANTINE AND HEALTH CERTIFICATION IN ASIA

John Humphrey
J. Richard Arthur
Rohana p. Subasinghe
Michael J. Phillips

Reprinted by arrangement with the
Food and Agriculture Organization of the United Nations

by

Daya Publishing House

A Division of

Astral International Pvt Ltd

New Delhi - 110 002

"This book was originally published by the Food and Agriculture Organization of the United Nations (FAO) as Vaccine Manual, FAO Animal Production and Health Series No. 35".

"The designations employed and the presentation of material in this publication do not imply the expression of any opinion, whatsoever on the part of the Food and Agriculture Organization of the United Nations concerning the legal status of any country, territory, city or area or of its authorities, or concerning the delimitations of its frontiers or boundaries."

'The designations 'developed' and 'developing' economies are intended for statistical convenience and do not necessarily express a judgment about the stage reached by a particular country, territory or area in the development process.'

First Indian Edition, 2005
Reprinted, 2024
ISBN: 978-81-70353-90-4

Published by : **Daya Publishing House**
A Division of
Astral International Pvt Ltd
4736/23, Ansari Road
Darya Ganj, New Delhi - 110002
Phone: 011-43549197
Email: info@astralint.com
Web: www.astralint.com

Printed at : **Chawla Offset Printers,** Delhi-110 052

Preparation of this Document

This document contains the technical papers presented at the Regional Workshop on Health and Quarantine Guidelines for the Responsible Movement (Introduction and Transfer) of Aquatic Organisms, held in Bangkok, Thailand, January 1996, selected background documents prepared by FAO, and the recommendations of the workshop. The workshop was held in collaboration with the Network of Aquaculture Centres in Asia-Pacific (NACA), the Aquatic Animal Health Research Institute of the Thai Department of Fisheries (AAHRI) and the Australian Center for International Agricultural Research (ACIAR), and was attended by representatives of a number of regional governments, institutions and agencies, and international organizations.

Distribution:

FAO Fisheries Department
FAO Regional Fisheries and Aquaculture Officers
FAO field projects
Directorates of Fisheries
Fish Health Institutions of the Asia-Pacific
Other interested parties
Participants

Humphrey, J.; Arthur, J.R.; Subasinghe, R.P.; Phillips, M.J.
Aquatic animal quarantine and health certification in Asia. Proceedings of the Regional Workshop on Health and Quarantine Guidelines for the Responsible Movement (Introduction and Transfer) of Aquatic Organisms. Bangkok, Thailand, 28 January 1996.
FAO Fisheries Technical Paper. No. 373. Rome, FAO. 1997. 153p.

ABSTRACT

Quarantine programmes form part of a first line of defense against possible adverse effects resulting from the trans-boundary movement of aquatic species. Although "Codes of Practice" for the international movement of aquatic animals have been developed by various international organizations, they have been rarely applied in many countries. Nevertheless, they provide a starting point for designing national and regional fish health regulations, as well as international agreements aimed at preventing the spread of aquatic animal pathogens. Articles 9.3.2 and 9.3.3 of the Code of Conduct for Responsible Fisheries call for international cooperation in the elaboration, adoption and implementation of international Codes of Practice and procedures for introductions and transfers of aquatic organisms, and resolution 4/95 of the Twenty-eighth Session of the FAO Conference on 31 October 1995 requests FAO to assist in facilitating the preparation and implementation of appropriate national Codes of Practice and procedures to this effect. In recognition of these recommendations, assistance is being provided to the countries of Asia to formulate technical guidelines on health certification and quarantine for the responsible trans-boundary movement of aquatic animals. FAO, in collaboration with the Network of Aquaculture Centres in Asia-Pacific (NACA), the Aquatic Animal Health Research Institute of the Thai Department of Fisheries (AAHRI) and the Australian Center for International Agricultural Research (ACIAR) conducted a workshop in January 1996 in Bangkok, Thailand, with the view to review the existing knowledge on aquatic animal quarantine and health certification in Asia, and to develop an agreed-upon strategy for the formulation of technical guidelines. This document contains ten country papers presented at the workshop, some technical background information on general principles of aquatic animal quarantine, existing Codes of Practice, the agreed-upon strategy, and the recommendations of the workshop.

(Key words: Asia, Pacific, Aquaculture, Health certification, Fish disease, Quarantine)

Contents

Page

SECTION 1: BACKGROUND TO THE WORKSHOP

Introduction

The Code of Conduct on Responsible Fisheries has been approved and agreed upon by the FAO member countries at the twenty-eighth Session of the FAO Conference (20 October to 2 November 1995, Rome). The Articles 9.3.2 and 9.3.3, respectively state that *"States should cooperate in the elaboration, adoption and implementation of international codes of practice and procedures for introductions and transfers of aquatic organisms"* and *"States should, in order to minimize risks of disease transfer and other adverse effects on wild and cultured stocks, encourage adoption of appropriate practices in the genetic improvement of broodstocks, the introduction of non-native species, and in the production, sale and transport of eggs, larvae or fry, broodstock or other live materials. States should facilitate the preparation and implementation of appropriate national codes of practice and procedures to this effect"* (FAO, 1995). In order to facilitate development of national codes of practice on health certification and quarantine for aquatic animals and animal products, as a response to the requests made by the FAO member countries, Fisheries Department of FAO embarked upon an activity to develop a global document on Practical Guidelines for the Responsible Movement (Introduction and Transfer) of Aquatic Organisms.

The Network of Aquaculture Centres in Asia and the Pacific (NACA) has recognized the regional importance of aquatic animal health management and the role of aquatic animal quarantine. A program to develop and implement aquatic animal health management has been incorporated into the second five year work program of NACA (NACA, 1996). At the request of member countries, the NACA Governing Council recommended the drafting and adoption of regional guidelines for health certification and quarantine of aquatic animals in the Asia-Pacific region. Responding to needs for the development and adoption of minimum aquatic animal health certification and quarantine for the Region, and the recommendation of the NACA Governing Council, FAO in collaboration with NACA and the Aquatic Animal Health Research Institute in Thailand (AAHRI), a recognized regional center of excellence in aquatic animal health management, organized this workshop. The workshop was attended by participants from countries of the region and by representatives from a number of regional and international institutions, including FAO, NACA, Office International des Epizooties (OIE), Australian Center for International Agricultural Research (ACIAR), Asian Fisheries Society and AAHRI. The workshop program is given in Annex I and the list of participants is given in Annex II.

Objectives of the workshop

The main objective of the workshop was to review and evaluate the current status of knowledge and the ongoing initiatives (national, regional and global) on aquatic animal health certification and quarantine, which have relevance to Asia, and to develop a strategy for implementation of an Asia regional program to formulate technical guidelines on health certification and quarantine for the responsible trans-boundary movement of aquatic animals in Asia. In doing so, the practical applicability of the existing international codes on aquatic animal health and quarantine, including those of the OIE, the European Inland Fisheries Advisory Commission (EIFAC) and the International Council for the Exploration of the Sea (ICES) was also examined.

Background

Since 1984, world aquaculture production has increased from 10.5 million tonnes to 25.46 million tonnes in 1994, with an average compounded growth rate of nine percent per year. During this period, freshwater finfish production increased steadily while relatively high value crustacean production showed a comparatively rapid growth. The total contribution of aquaculture production to global fisheries increased significantly (9.6% per year) during this period, as did the value of aquaculture production (from US$ 13 billion to 39.83 billion) (FAO/FIDI, 1996). Considering the present rate of population expansion and in keeping with the present average global per caput fish consumption of 13 kg/year, it has been estimated that the global demand for fish and shellfish may be in the order of 87 million tonnes by the year 2010 (FAO/Japan, 1995). In order to meet this predicted demand, the global aquaculture production would have to be doubled over the next 15 years.

Asia is at the forefront of aquaculture production, both in terms of volume and value. China, India and Japan alone account for 65% percent of world production. Asian aquaculture production comes from a number of different aquaculture systems ranging from intensive and semi-intensive systems to extensive systems and culture-based fisheries. Aquaculture in Asia holds considerable potential for further growth, through intensification, diversification and further expansion. However, if this potential is to be realized, Asian aquaculture must grow in a responsible and sustainable manner (ADB/NACA, 1996). In particular, one of the most significant constraints that will re-emerge during this process of growth is the threat of disease (ADB/NACA, 1996). With intensification, aquaculture systems have to rely heavily on external inputs such as seed and feed. This will pose further threats of introduction of pathogens into aquaculture systems. An understanding of ways of dealing with such situations will become significant for the sustainability of aquaculture. Establishing effective quarantine guidelines and health certification procedures is a way forward to minimizing risk of introduction of pathogens.

Quarantine programs form part of a first line of defense against possible adverse effects resulting from the trans-boundary movement of aquatic species. As such, they must be developed within the context of larger national and international plans addressing this problem. "Codes of Practice" for the international movement of aquatic species which have been developed by international organizations provide a starting point for designing national and regional fish health legislation as well as international agreements aiming at preventing the spread of disease-causing pathogens. To succeed, the development of regionally agreed-upon lists of notifiable pathogens, the standardization of diagnostic techniques and the production of health certificates of unambiguous meaning must accompany such efforts. A strong commitment by aquafarmers and governments and the cooperation of importers and exporters as well as seed producers and traders are considered key elements in the success of these programs. Successful disease prevention may also be directly related to (i) the ability of countries to reduce their dependence on imported broodstock and fry for the aquaculture industry, and (ii) to regulation of shipments for the ornamental fish trade, particularly those involving wild-caught fishes (Arthur, 1995).

Regional approach

The development, adoption and implementation of uniform regional aquatic animal health certification and quarantine practices in the Asian-Pacific region must be viewed as a long-term goal because of:

- Differences in existing quarantine legislation, policies and practices between countries in the region.
- The magnitude and socio-economic importance of trade in living aquatic animals and their products.
- The diversity of species and purposes for which aquatic animals and their products are traded.
- Reliance of fisheries-related industries based on movements of aquatic animals/products.
- Dependence on trade in aquatic animals/products for the livelihood of many people.
- Limited laboratory capabilities for evaluating health status of imported animals in many countries.
- Limited quarantine facilities for holding imported animals.
- Possible difficulties in certain countries to adopt improved quarantine practices.
- Possible reluctance by industry to adopt changes to existing practices.
- The limited disease occurrence and distribution data on which to formulate and implement quarantine.

Previous regional recommendations

Recognition of the need to develop, adopt and implement regional quarantine and health certification programs is not new. Fundamental guidelines and principles for aquatic animal quarantine for the Asian-Pacific Region have been developed in a number of papers, workshops and reports over the past two decades (ADB/NACA, 1991, Arthur, 1987 & 1995, Copland and Lucas, 1988, Davy and Chouinard, 1983, Davy and Graham, 1979, Morschel, 1988, and Roberts, 1981). Davy and Chouinard (1983) have emphasized the need for caution with respect to disease incursions in considering introductions of aquatic animals in the region.

A number of general principles arising from the above activities have been proposed for consideration, adoption and implementation in the Asian-Pacific region, including:

- Establishment and implementation of quarantine for aquatic animals (as for other animals) in order that current and new enterprises based on aquatic animal species, and such species in the natural aquatic environment, will be protected from introduced pathogens.
- Establishment of a central fish disease laboratory with high level diagnostic capabilities and information support to identify and characterize pathogens, parasites and diseases of aquatic animals and assist in recommending treatment and control measures.
- Establishment of quarantine controls consistent with international and regional standards to facilitate trade and movements of aquatic animals and their products between countries and within the region.
- Specific health certification by exporters to provide a reliable measure of surety that protocols for movements have been followed.
- Inspection and laboratory examination of imported fish to verify the health of such animals and to identify and restrict entry of diseased animals.
- Treatment and observation of fish in quarantine as necessary to prevent the introduction of pathogens or parasites responsive to treatment and to ensure the introduction of healthy stock.
- Use of quarantine operational procedures which mitigate against disease incursion by:
    - water filtration prior to discharge to prevent escape of potential pathogens or pests;
    - safe disposal of water after transfer to prevent against escape of pathogens;
    - destruction of stock with diseases or predators; and

- sterilization of all equipment.

- Approved quarantine premises to promote a high level of microbiological security through the holding of aquatic animals under appropriate conditions and with appropriate facilities for treatment and disposal of water.
- Transfer of eggs or young stages, as in general, these stages carry fewer pathogens than mature animals, and in some cases may be disinfected to reduce further the risk of disease incursion.
- Introductions from within the natural distribution range of the species to mitigate against exotic pathogen or pest introduction.
- Safe disposal of imported transport water and the accompanying pests to minimize the inadvertent introduction of pathogens, parasites, pests or diseases which may accompany shipments of aquatic animals.
- Sanitary surveillance of fish farms in order to provide a high level of surety of disease freedom prior to export.
- Pre and post-transfer quarantine, assurance of disease freedom, and pre-import sanitary certification to increase the probability of freedom from disease.
- The inclusion of fish and lower animals into existing quarantine legislation, as such animals are notorious vectors of infectious disease and must be subject to quarantine practices similar to those used for higher aquatic and terrestrial animals.
- Penalties for non-compliance to mitigate against illegal or undesirable practices which may result in disease incursions.
- Powers to seize and destroy to prevent intentional or unintentional release of diseased stock
- Identification of major infectious agents and quarantine precautions required to prevent the spread of such agents. Listings of high and low risk agents should be available on a regional basis to assist in quarantine decisions.
- Establishment of a regional center for information on diseases and quarantine procedures to assist in the development and implementation of aquatic animal quarantine and health certification procedures.
- Certification of compliance, declarations and inspections by a competent exporting authority to provide a high level of surety and compliance.
- Designated ports of entry to assist in quarantine inspection and procedures.
- Holding, treatment and release from quarantine under the jurisdiction of quarantine officials to ensure compliance with protocols and to ensure release of healthy individuals.

Socio-economic importance of diseases

The economic impact of disease on the aquaculture industries of Asia is substantial. According to estimates made in 1990, diseases of fish and other aquatic animals accounted for at least US $1.36 billion in losses. Actual annual losses may be two or more times this estimate. The recent ADB/NACA Regional Study on Aquaculture Sustainability and Environment estimated, through farm level surveys, that financial losses from disease and other environment problems may exceed US$ 3 billion per year (ADB/NACA, 1996).

The collapse of the shrimp industry of Taiwan Province of China in the late 1990s saw its share of Asian shrimp production drop from 21% to 4%, one of the painful experiences of the recent past. Similar events also occurred in Thailand, China, India, Cambodia and Bangladesh, with tremendous losses to their shrimp culture industries. In marine fish culture, Japanese losses in 1992 for the most important species amounted to US$ 114.4 million or about 5.7% of total production. In Southeast Asia, diseases in cage-cultured grouper, snapper and seabass in Malaysia cost growers US$ 1.3 million in potential income in 1982 alone. In 1990 an outbreak of vibriosis in sea-cage farms in Malaysia cost farmers MR 20 million, and more recent losses have amounted to MR 6-10 million per year. In Thailand, losses of marine cage-cultured seabass and grouper in 1989 were on the order of US$ 1.9 million. These estimates indicate the important role diseases play in determining the economic success or failure of fish culture operations. In freshwater, epizootic ulcerative syndrome (EUS) has had severe social and economic impacts in rural fish farming and fishing communities, with losses in several Asian countries of tens of millions of US$ (Lilley et al., 1992).

Way forward

Despite recommendations in support of enhanced regional quarantine measures, protection of national fisheries resources by quarantine and health certification procedures have not been universally accepted. The well recognized and documented incursions of aquatic animal disease associated with introductions and transfers of living aquatic animals, and adverse social, economic and environmental impacts which can arise from such incursions, suggest governments should recognize the risks of uncontrolled entry of living aquatic animals and adopt appropriate measures. Such issues are likely to assume greater importance in the face of rapid expansion and increased future reliance on aquaculture and other fisheries industries.

Countries of the Asian-Pacific region have many social, economic, industrial, environmental, biological and geographical factors in common. This commonality logically favors the adoption and implementation of regional quarantine practices and aquatic animal health certification that would be expected to facilitate trade and offer enhanced protection of industry and the environment from incursions of disease. This has been recognized by the governments of NACA, who have requested the development and dissemination of guidelines and protocols for improvements in quarantine measures for controlling the impacts of uncontrolled spread of aquatic animals on indigenous aquaculture industries and fisheries (NACA, 1996). This present workshop is an important step forward to some specific actions on this important subject.

SECTION 2: THE WORKSHOP

Opening ceremony

Speakers in the Opening Session each stressed the importance of disease control in aquaculture and the importance of addressing disease issues through programs of aquatic animal health management. It was emphasized that a program for aquatic animal health management was part of the next 5 year initiative of NACA, that this FAO initiative had a important role in providing NACA with advice on how to implement quarantine and health certification, and that NACA was looking to responding to the advice of the Workshop. The detailed technical program of the workshop is in Annex I. The speeches made at the opening ceremony are given in Annex III and IV.

Presentation of country reports

Each invited participant presented an overview of current quarantine and health certification procedures and requirements for their country. The detailed country papers are given in Annex V. The following summarizes the general issues that emerged:

- Differences between countries in legislation and requirements for imports and exports of living aquatic animals and aquatic animal products.
- A need for guidelines and advice on aquatic animal health certification and quarantine.
- The establishment, in some countries, of committees to address and provide advice on aquatic animal health and quarantine.
- A need for training and human resources in aquatic animal health and quarantine.
- A need for infrastructure: quarantine and laboratory facilities.
- Recognition of a need for appropriate legislation.
- Recognition of the social and economic importance of aquaculture, fisheries production and trade in aquatic animals and aquatic animal products, including ornamental fish.
- Concerns by some countries regarding spread of zoonotic diseases via aquatic animal and their products.
- Recognition of the existence of farming and trade in a diverse range of aquatic animals, including frogs, turtles, echinoderms and other such species.
- The use of veterinary diagnostic laboratories for fish diseases in some countries.
- Lack of regional guidelines or consensus on diseases of significance.

Workshop discussion

A number of important points relating to developing a strategy for the development and implementation of health certification and quarantine guidelines were made during the workshop discussion including:

- The need to define quarantine and health certification and to use these terms in an unambiguous manner.
- The importance of involving the aquaculture industry/private sector.
- The need to establish a timeframe for the implementation of improved quarantine measures. There should be a progressive implementation and adoption of the guidelines. It was recognized that to push too hard would be counterproductive. It was also desirable to move towards common acceptable guidelines for the region.
- The need to clearly specify aquatic animals and aquatic animal products in discussions to avoid confusion with domestic (terrestrial) animals and products. It was suggested that the strategy should concentrate only on disease, and that environmental and biodiversity issues (e.g., as related to the introduction of exotics) should be considered separately.
- The need to incorporate aquatic animals other than finfish, molluscs and crustaceans into regional aquatic animal health certification and quarantine considerations. There are a wide range of species to consider, including animals such as frogs and seacucumbers.
- The importance of adopting and utilizing, where possible, existing OIE codes and guidelines. The workshop was appraised of the links between international trade and what is acceptable now in animal health certification requirements of importing countries as a result of the Sanitary, Phyto-sanitary (SPS) Agreement reached during the latest GATT round. From now on, under the new World Trade Organisation (WTO), the only acceptable international health requirement standards affecting trade in animals (including aquatic animals) are those laid down in the OIE code. It was recognized that the OIE code was heavily geared towards Europe and North America. Some aspects of the OIE code as it now stands were considered inappropriate for the Asian-Pacific region, and there was therefore a need to revise guidelines to make them more applicable to the region. An annual revision of the OIE Aquatic Animal Health Code may be appropriate.
- The need for flexibility in formulating strategies and adopting health certification and quarantine practices and procedures.
- The importance of collaborating with and assisting regional countries in developing aquatic animal health certification and quarantine guidelines. A 'national coordinator' could be appointed in each country participating in the process of developing the regional guidelines. The National Coordinator would

be responsible for coordination of activities at the national level, and would act as a link to regional efforts.

- A regional working group should be established as part of the regional quarantine strategy, which would interact closely with the national coordinators for development of the guidelines.
- Understanding the concept of risk evaluation, whereby different risks associated with different products and circumstances warrant differing levels of health certification and quarantine. The importance of defining 'acceptable' risk was emphasized.
- The lack of communication between fisheries and veterinary authorities in transmission of disease data to OIE. The need to involve fisheries departments and agencies in the collection of fish disease information was strongly emphasized, particularly as veterinarians are less involved in aquatic animal disease in the Asia-Pacific region. The workshop recognized the need to better organize the communication channels for exchange of information on aquatic animal diseases. The willingness of the OIE Fish Disease Commission to receive submissions from any competent organization or individual was mentioned.

Fundamental principles for regional quarantine

As a basis for developing a strategy for implementing a regional program to develop guidelines for aquatic animals health certification and quarantine, a number of fundamental principles were presented to the workshop for consideration. These were discussed and agreed upon. The amended principles are presented in Annex VI.

Proposed regional strategy

The workshop then discussed in detail the proposed regional strategy for the development and implementation of health and quarantine guidelines for the responsible movement (introduction and transfer) of aquatic organisms. The revised strategy, based on the discussions and recommendations of the workshop, is given as Annex VII. The following are the main points arising during the discussions:

- FAO has been instrumental in drafting a Code of Practice for the introduction of aquatic animals in the region, which is consistent with international standards but focused on the needs, and capabilities of the Asian region. Similarly, NACA has identified as a high priority the development of aquatic animal health certification and the implementation of quarantine for the region to achieve similar goals.
- A Regional Working Group (RWG) on Aquatic Animal Health and Quarantine should be formed as a starting point to initiate the strategy. The RWG would be responsible for liaison with all parties involved and for the ongoing development, circulation, revision and promotion of regional aquatic animal health certification

and quarantine guidelines. The RWG would also assume a role in collation of disease data, collation of current quarantine policies and practices, and would provide advice on disease diagnostic procedures. As such, the RWG would act as a regional specialist resource on diseases and quarantine for aquatic animals.

- The RWG group should be based within a recognized regional organization with diverse experience and research interests in fisheries sciences and strong representation and support by regional countries. The Network of Aquaculture Centres in Asia-Pacific (NACA) is well placed to provide organizational and infrastructure support for the RWG, and a central role of NACA in the strategy was accepted by the Workshop. The RWG should be developed in active partnership with FAO. FAO was requested to assist in the development of the group. The importance of linking in with OIE (with which NACA had an MOU) and of the active participation of regional governments, academic experts and the aquaculture industry was emphasized, as was the importance of involving legal expertise.
- A fish health expert would be appointed by NACA as part of the new 5-year work program of NACA, and that such an individual could play an important role in providing coordination to the RWG and assisting in implementation of the regional strategy.
- The workshop considered that the regional activities should be closely linked into a global effort to reduce the impacts of aquatic animal diseases, and an "Ad hoc Advisory Group on Aquaculture Health Management" should be established at the global level. The group should mainly consist of responsible officers from FAO and OIE. The committee should seek participation from other concerned international organizations and institutions as seen appropriate.
- The workshop emphasized the importance of linking with OIE Fish Diseases Commission on reporting of the aquatic animal disease outbreaks in the region.
- The workshop considered the participation of the Pacific region in the initiative, and it was suggested South Pacific Commission (SPC) is an important agency to coordinate efforts among the Pacific countries. It was considered premature to include all Pacific countries at this stage. Cooperation between SPC and NACA should be encouraged for the dissemination of information to the Pacific countries.
- A regional workshop to specifically introduce the concept of regional aquatic animal health certification and quarantine was seen essential, with the opportunity for each regional country to present issues, problems and needs relating to certification and quarantine. Representation and involvement of industry groups at such a workshop will assist in eliciting industry awareness and support for the strategy.

- A regional meeting specifically to discuss minimal quarantine guidelines involving all interested parties, especially representatives from all key agencies or departments of regional countries should be held. The agenda for the meeting should be clearly spelt out, i.e. the meeting is to seek formal agreement and adoption in principle of the minimal quarantine guidelines by those government representatives present. It was emphasized that representatives should be clear that acceptance and adoption of the minimal guidelines at the meeting does not constitute adoption by their respective governments. Rather, it is adoption in principle by regional experts and authorities of the principles. At some point subject to satisfactory collaboration and revision, formal ratification and adoption in principle by members of regional countries is necessary.

- The ultimate objective of the strategy is to develop a set of guidelines for appropriate regional aquatic animal health and quarantine and certification that could be used to prepare legislation of regional countries such that a regional uniformity exists. This does not mean that each country should have the same legislation. Rather, individual legislation should provide for common practices and uniformity to facilitate regional trade and movements of aquatic animals and aquatic animal products.

- ACIAR agreed to assist the strategy by training a selected group of regional fish health experts on epidemiology and data collection through a trainer-training program. ACIAR envisages to develop a program to support in-country training programs using the trainees of the previous program who are now considered as trainers. The workshop welcomed this assistance from ACIAR.

- FAO will provide assistance to the strategy by identifying developing and testing a computer database program for this purpose. FAO will also provide support for collecting data from the countries in the region through appointing person in the regional countries to collect data through TCDC mechanism. The workshop welcomed this assistance from FAO.

Workshop closing remarks

Dr Banchong Tiensongrusmee, NACA Coordinator, thanked all for their attendance, and informed the participants that the NACA secretariat would follow up with the recommendations.

Dr Rohana Subasinghe said that FAO would support the outcome of the meeting and that FAO would assist in achieving the objectives of the region. He thanked all for their contribution.

A technical meeting specifically to discuss national quarantine procedures in [illegible] interested [illegible] countries [illegible] of key agencies of [illegible] of regional countries should be held. The agenda for the meeting should be clearly [illegible] the meeting is to [illegible] and recommend [illegible] of the regional quarantine guidelines by these international government agencies. [illegible] It was emphasized that [illegible] should be clear that acceptance and adoption of the regional guidelines at the meeting does not constitute [illegible] binding to [illegible] governments. Rather it is advisory in principle to [illegible] governments and authorities of the countries. At some point [illegible] would be [illegible] national legislation and [illegible] before [illegible] would be considered to be accepted.

The ultimate [illegible] of the [illegible] is to [illegible] guidelines for [illegible] regional [illegible] and [illegible] quarantine [illegible] need to [illegible] of the national [illegible] that a regional [illegible]. This does not mean that each country should have the same [illegible]. Rather [illegible] should [illegible] to [illegible] and [illegible] regional technical [illegible] as [illegible].

[illegible] FAO and [illegible] to assist the [illegible] training of [illegible] that [illegible] and [illegible] through [illegible] training programme [illegible] to develop [illegible] of [illegible] country training programmes [illegible] and [illegible] for [illegible] assistance from ACIAR.

FAO will provide assistance to [illegible] in identifying, developing and [illegible] for this purpose. FAO will also provide support for [illegible] in the region [illegible]. [illegible] welcomed this assistance from FAO.

[illegible] closing remarks

Dr. [illegible], [illegible] NACA [illegible], thanked all the [illegible] and [illegible] participants [illegible] recommendations.

Dr. [illegible] said that FAO would support the [illegible] meeting and [illegible] would [illegible] the objectives of the region. He thanked [illegible] for their contribution.

ANNEX I: WORKSHOP PROGRAM

Session I: Opening ceremony

0830-0900	Registration
0900-0910	Welcome address by Dr Banchong Tiensongrusmee, NACA Coordinator
0910-0920	Speech by Dr Rohana Subasinghe, FIRI/FAO
0920-0930	Keynote address by Dr Plodprasop Suraswadi, Director-General, Department of Fisheries, Thailand

Session II: Presentation of country reports

0930-0945	Bangladesh
0945-1000	Cambodia
1000-1015	China
1015-1030	India
1030-1100	Break for refreshments
1100-1115	Indonesia
1115-1130	Japan
1130-1145	Malaysia
1145-1200	Nepal
1200-1215	Philippines
1215-1230	Thailand
1230	Break for lunch

Session III: Discussion session

1400-1410	Introductory remarks
1410-1530	Discussion session
1530-1600	Break for refreshments
1600-1800	Discussion session (continued)
1800	Close of workshop

ANNEX II: LIST OF WORKSHOP PARTICIPANTS

Dr. Mohammad Abdul Hossain Chief Scientific Officer, Marine Station, Fisheries Research Institute, Motel Road, Cox's Bazar, BANGLADESH	Tel: (880-341) 3855
Ms. Cen Feng Deputy Director, Fish Diseases Prevention Division, National Station of Fisheries Technical Extension, Ministry of Agriculture, Nongzhanguan Nanli, Beijing, PEOPLES REPUBLIC OF CHINA	Fax: (86-10) 4192961, 5002448
Dr. Punyabrata Das Director, National Bureau of Fish Genetic Resources, 351/28 Dariapur, Talkatora Road, Lucknow-226004, INDIA	Fax: (91-522) 259 820 Tel: (91-522) 259 315
Dr. Hariyadi Mangunwiryo Central Research Institute for Fisheries, Jl. K.S. Tubun, Slipi, Jakarta 11410A, INDONESIA	Fax: (62-21) 570 9159
Dr. Kazuhiro Nakajima Senior Researcher, National Research Institute of Aquaculture, 422-1 Nansei-cho, Watarai-gun, Mie 519-04, JAPAN	Fax: (81-5996) 6 1962 Tel: (81-5996) 6 1830

Dr. Ismail Awang Kechick Fisheries Research Officer Fisheries Research Institute, Ministry of Agriculture Batu Maung, Penang MALAYSIA	Fax: (60-3) 626 2210 Tel: (60-3) 626 5925
Mr. Gopal B. Shrestha Fisheries Development Division Department of Agriculture Central Fisheries Building Balaju, Kathmandu NEPAL	Fax: (977-1) 272 833 Tel: (977-1) 270 609
Dr. Melba Reantaso Senior Aquaculturist Bureau of Fisheries and Aquatic Resources Quezon Avenue, Quezon City Metro Manila 3008 PHILIPPINES	Fax: (63-2) 98 78 71 Tel: (63-2) 98 85 17
Dr. Pornlerd Chanratchakool Aquatic Animal Health Research Institute Department of Fisheries, Kasetsart University Campus Ladyao, Jatujak, Bangkok 10900 THAILAND	Fax: (66-2) 561 3993 Tel: (66-2) 579 6803
Dr. John Humphrey Biodata Resources Pty. Ltd. 8 Karli Gardens, Yarrawonga, Victoria 3730 AUSTRALIA	Fax: (61-57) 43 2515 E-mail: humphreyj@woody.agvic.gov.au
Mr. B. Smith Research Programme Co-ordinator ACIAR Fisheries Programme Box 21, Cronulla NSW 2230 AUSTRALIA	Fax: (61-2) 523 5966 Tel: (61-2) 527 8463 E-mail: smithb@fisheries.nsw.gov.au

Prof. Mohd Shariff Faculty of Veterinary Medicine Universiti Putra Malaysia UPM, Serdang, Selangor Darul Ehsan MALAYSIA	Fax: (60-3) 948 8246 Tel: (60-3) 948 8246 E-mail: shariff@vet.upm.edu.my
Mr. Jorgen G. Jensen Chief of Agriculture, Irrigation, Forestry and Fisheries Unit Secretariat, Mekong River Commission Kasatsuk Bridge, Rama I Road, Bangkok 10330 THAILAND	Fax: (66-2) 225 2796 Tel: (66-2) 225 0029
Dr. Barry J. Hill Head, Fish Disease Laboratory Ministry of Agriculture Fisheries and Food Albany Road, Grandby Industrial Estate Weymouth, Dorset DT4 9TH UNITED KINGDOM	Fax: (44-1305) 206 601 Tel: (44-1305) 206 626 E-mail: b.j.hill@cefas.co.uk
Prof. Chen Shu Nan National University of Taiwan No. 1, Roosvelt Road, Section 4, Taipei, Taiwan 10764 TAIWAN REPUBLIC OF CHINA	Fax: (886) 23687122
Prof. William Howarth Eliot College University of Kent at Canterbury Kent CT2 7NS UNITED KINGDOM	Fax: (44-1227) 827 831 Tel: (44-1227) 823 341
Dr. Richard Arthur Head, Parasitology Section Department of Fisheries and Oceans Maurice Lamontagne Institute Mont-Joli, QC, Victoria 3730 CANADA G5H 3Z4	Fax: (1-418) 775 0542 Tel: (1-418) 775 0640 E-mail: rarthur@cancom.net

Dr. Rohana Subasinghe Fishery Resources Officer (Fish Health), Inland Water Resources and Aquaculture Service, Fisheries Department Food and Agriculture Organization of the United Nations (FAO), Via Delle Terme di Caracalla, Rome 00100 ITALY	Fax: (39-6) 570 53020 Tel: (39-6) 570 56473 E-mail: rohana.subasinghe@fao.org
Dr. Kamonporn Tonguthai Director, Aquatic Animal Health Research Institute Department of Fisheries Kasetsart University Campus Ladyao, Jatujak, Bangkok 10900 THAILAND	Fax: (66-2) 561 3993 Tel: (66-2) 579 4122 E-mail: aahri@ksc.net.th
Mr. Ian MacRae SEAADCP/Aquatic Animal Health Research Institute Department of Fisheries Kasetsart University Campus Ladyao, Jatujak, Bangkok 10900 THAILAND	Fax: (66-2) 561 3993 Tel: (66-2) 579 4122 E-mail: aahri@ksc.net.th
Dr. Banchong Tiensongrusmee Co-ordinator Network of Aquaculture Centres in Asia-Pacific Department of Fisheries Compound, Kasetsart University Campus Ladyao, Jatujak, Bangkok 10900 THAILAND	Fax: (66-2) 561 1727 Tel: (66-2) 561 1728 to 9 E-mail: naca@mozart.inet.co.th.

Mr. Hassanai Kongkeo Senior Aquaculturist Network of Aquaculture Centres in Asia-Pacific Department of Fisheries Compound, Kasetsart University Campus Ladyao, Jatujak, Bangkok 10900 THAILAND	Fax: (66-2) 561 1727 Tel: (66-2) 561 1728 to 9 E-mail: naca@mozart.inet.co.th
Mr. Pedro Bueno Information Specialist Network of Aquaculture Centres in Asia-Pacific Department of Fisheries Compound, Kasetsart University Campus Ladyao, Jatujak, Bangkok 10900 THAILAND	Fax: (66-2) 561 1727 Tel: (66-2) 561 1728 to 9 E-mail: naca@mozart.inet.co.th
Dr. Michael J. Phillips Environment Specialist Network of Aquaculture Centres in Asia-Pacific Department of Fisheries, Kasetsart University Campus Ladyao, Jatujak, Bangkok 10900 THAILAND	Fax: (66-2) 561 1727 Tel: (66-2) 561 1728 to 9 E-mail: naca@mozart.inet.co.th

ANNEX III: KEYNOTE ADDRESS

Dr Plodprasop Suraswadi
Director-General,
Department of Fisheries, Thailand

Distinguished delegates, ladies and gentlemen, good morning. I would like to extend to you, on behalf of the Government of Thailand, a very warm welcome to this workshop. We thank you for the privilege of hosting this event; we are honoured by your presence and hope you will find the meeting both educational and enjoyable.

Thailand can offer many lessons on aquaculture development and is keenly interested in the topic of the workshop. As many of you are aware, aquaculture in Thailand has developed very rapidly in recent years, and has contributed a great deal to the social and economic development of the country. The policy of the Thai government is to continue to strengthen the development of aquaculture, and we expect to see further sustainable advances in the production of shrimp, fish and other aquatic species in the years to come.

Much of the recent expansion has been in coastal aquaculture, and Thailand has now become the world's leading producer of shrimp, generating over $1.5 billion dollars per year for the export earnings of the country. Whilst shrimp farming has brought enormous earnings for the country, and the creation of ancillary industries which have generated more economic activity, particularly in coastal areas, the rapid expansion of shrimp farming has led to some environmental and shrimp disease problems. The Thai government has been actively dealing with these problems, and has made great strides in the control of shrimp diseases. Nevertheless, the problems of shrimp and fish disease are important ones which will continue to affect the sustainability of aquaculture industries, affecting large and small-scale farmers alike. This is an area where we must be increasingly diligent and active in research, training of our staff and farmers, extension and in responsible management of our aquaculture industry.

One of the potential sources of new diseases is from the uncontrolled movement of aquatic animals, and this is an area where we must be particularly vigilant. The Thai government has been active for some time with programmes designed to control the introduction of undesirable species through quarantine measures. Nevertheless, at this time of increased economic activity and expanding trade between countries of the region, and between regions, it is important to seek ways to ensure that such trade does not bring increased risk to our aquaculture industry from the introduction of new pathogens and fish or shrimp diseases. It is for this reason that we in the Government look forward to the results of this important workshop, and are keenly interested to participate in follow up activities. We expect the workshop to lead to some effective programme of action that will provide quarantine and health guidelines for the responsible movement of aquatic animals. I encourage you, the participants, to work hard and consider your options carefully. The guidelines should seek to meet identified risks but be practical and workable in their implementation. I would also encourage you to look further than just guidelines. Guidelines are useful to our government, and we look forward with interest to the outcome of your deliberations. However, I urge you to consider further the means of implementation of the guidelines, and of other activities that can be taken up, such as training, research actions, infrastructure development and extension activities, all of which may be required in a comprehensive programme for the development of practical methods to reduce risks associated with uncontrolled spread of aquatic animal diseases. I can assure you that Thailand looks forward to the active participation in the follow up from this workshop.

I would like to thank FAO for its timely support for this workshop and NACA for effectively co-ordinating its implementation, in close co-operation with the Aquatic Animal Health Research Institute (AAHRI) of the Royal Thai Government. As you know, Thailand hosted the NACA project which has now evolved into the independent intergovernmental NACA. Through this, and with the active involvement of the Department of Fisheries and its various institutes involved in aquaculture and fisheries development, Thailand has shown its strong adherence to regional co-operation in aquaculture development. I would like to take this opportunity to re-affirm Thailand's strong support to regional co-operation.

I am also pleased to learn that this is one of the activities being identified under the new 5-year Work Programme of NACA, which has the theme of Aquaculture Sustainability. I must congratulate the NACA Secretariat on taking quick action on the implementation of this work programme, following its approval during last October's Governing Council meeting. The Thai government looks forward to working further with NACA in the implementation of this important regional programme. I would also like to thank our esteemed colleagues from the other governments for contributing their time to this workshop. I am also pleased to acknowledge the presence of several technical assistance agencies in this meeting. I would like to call on international and regional organisations to continue to work closely with governments in the follow up to this important workshop, particularly in the implementation of a regional programme to develop health guidelines and implement action programmes for the responsible movement of aquatic animals, which will I am sure contribute to the further sustainable development of our aquaculture industries.

Finally, I congratulate the organisers of the workshop, FAO, NACA and AAHRI, extend a warm welcome to all colleagues from other governments and my best wishes for a successful conclusion of the workshop. I look forward to learning in detail of the outcome of the workshop and I wish you all an enjoyable meeting and a pleasant stay in Thailand.

Thank you.

ANNEX IV: WELCOME ADDRESS

Dr Banchong Tiensongrusmee
NACA Coordinator,
Bangkok, Thailand

Dr Plodprasop Suraswadi, fellow participants, friends, ladies and gentlemen, on behalf of the NACA Organisation, I am very happy to welcome you to this regional workshop on Health and Quarantine Guidelines for Responsible Movement of Aquatic Organisms.

I would like to thank the Government of Thailand through Dr Plodprasop Suraswadi, for its continuing support of NACA and for hosting this workshop. Thank you also to Dr Kamonporn Tonguthai, Director of the Aquatic Animal Health Research Institute (AAHRI). It has been a pleasure for the NACA Secretariat to work with you in the organisation of this workshop; NACA looks forward to further co-operative activities together in the future. I would like to express NACA's gratitude to FAO for co-sponsoring this workshop. Thank you Dr Subasinghe for your personal attention to this joint activity. I would be grateful if you would convey the appreciation of NACA for this co-operation to the concerned authorities at FAO Headquarters. NACA looks forward to working closely with FAO in the implementation of the follow up from this workshop and to further strengthening our collaborative relations with FAO.

Thank you also to the resource persons, who have clearly put a considerable amount of hard work into the preparation of background documents for the meeting. I am sure these materials will provide a basis for much interesting discussion during the workshop, and ensure a viable follow up action.

I am pleased also to welcome the representatives of several concerned organisations, including OIE, ACIAR, the Mekong Commission and the Asian Fisheries Society. Thank you for contributing your expertise and experiences to this activity.

I extend my special acknowledgement to our distinguished delegates from governments, who have devoted their time -- in the spirit of regional collaboration -- to attend this workshop. NACA looks to working further with you in the follow up actions to be taken from this workshop.

This workshop is one of the activities under the new 5-year Work Programme of NACA, which is giving a high priority to aquatic animal health management. This programme, which has the theme of aquaculture sustainability, includes a component to assist governments and the private sector reduce risks and safeguard indigenous biodiversity and aquaculture industries from adverse impacts associated with the trans-boundary movements and introductions of aquatic species. I am pleased to report that this new NACA Work Programme was endorsed by the 7th

Governing Council meeting of NACA, held in Nepal last October, which gave a high priority to aquatic animal health management.

The NACA Work Programme is intended as a co-operative programme where concerned agencies can work together with NACA in assisting the region's further aquaculture development. I am pleased that FAO has shown an interest in co-operating with NACA on this important workshop, in an area where both organisations have mutual interests. The OIE has also expressed keen interest to cooperate with NACA in the control of aquatic animal diseases, and a joint OIE-NACA working group on fish diseases information systems is planned for April 1996.

The need for guidelines on fish disease control mechanisms, including quarantine systems, was identified during the ADB/NACA Regional Workshop on Fish Health Management which was held in Pusan, Republic of Korea, in 1990. The FAO/NACA Regional Workshop on the Environmental Assessment and Management of Aquaculture Development also recommended assistance to governments in the formulation of policy concerning the introduction and transfer of aquatic species. The issues highlighted in these aforementioned meetings, to be discussed in this workshop today, are becoming increasingly urgent: (i) because of the rapidly expanding trade and movement in aquatic animals, with its associated risks of spread of fish and shrimp pathogens; and (ii) the increasing awareness of the need to protect indigenous biodiversity highlighted in the Convention on Biological Diversity, of which many Asian countries are now signatories.

The NACA organisation looks forward to the outcome of this workshop, particularly the preliminary health and quarantine guidelines for responsible movement of aquatic animals, and the follow up programme for implementation of improved strategies for the responsible movement of aquatic animals. I can assure you that NACA will take the necessary follow up action on the recommendations.

Finally, I reiterate my warm greetings and welcome, and look forward to a successful workshop.

Thank you.

ANNEX V: COUNTRY PAPERS

Bangladesh

M.A. Hossain
Marine Station, Fisheries Research Institute
Cox's Bazar, Bangladesh

Abstract

Bangladesh introduced new species of fish from abroad as early as the late 1950s starting with tilapia (*Oreochromis mossambicus*). However, it was not until the country began to import large quantities of *Penaeus monodon* post larvae in 1995 that the Government became increasingly concerned about health certification and quarantine procedures for imported aquatic animals. While Bangladesh would like to adopt the necessary legislation and guidelines, the country's knowledge of fish disease is fragmented and incomplete. Disease testing facilities are almost absent and trained manpower in the field is limited. Therefore, a code of practice or set of rules, should be developed alongside the training of manpower and provision of facilities.

Introduction

During 1995, the Ministry of Fisheries and Livestock (MoFL), Government of Bangladesh, received several requests from fisheries scientists and environmentalists to introduce proper quarantine guidelines for the import of *Penaeus monodon* post larvae from neighboring countries. In the same year, supply of natural post larvae from coastal areas diminished. To satisfy the demand from shrimp farmers, several traders rushed to start importing post larvae. At that point, it was painfully discovered that Bangladesh had no health and quarantine guidelines for importing live aquatic animals.

Ironically, Bangladesh, or East Pakistan as it was formerly known, introduced new species of fish from abroad as early as the late 1950s. The process started with Mossambique tilapia (*Oreochromis mossambicus*) and was followed by Nile tilapia (*O. niloticus*), common carp (*Cyprinus carpio*), grass carp (*Ctenopharyngodon idella*), silver carp (*Hypopthalmichthys molitrix*), big head carp (*Aristichthys nobilis*), black carp (*Mylopharyngodon piceus*), Thai silvar barb (Barbodes *gonionotus*), mahaseer (*Tor tor*), North African catfish (*Clarias gariepinus*), sutchi catfish (*Pangasius sutchi*) and recently, post larvae of black tiger shrimp (*Penaeus monodon*).

International and in-country trade in aquatic organisms

Reportedly, Bangladesh has imported nearly 140 species of ornamental aquarium fish. A few live weed fish were exported from Bangladesh as tropical ornamentals, but no records on their number, volume or price are available. Bangladesh has traditionally exported live turtles and tortoises to neighboring India and, more recently, live wild crabs to India and elsewhere. But there exists no specific health and quarantine guidelines for the export of live aquatic animals.

In-country trade of live aquatic animals in Bangladesh is becoming increasingly popular due to the expansion of both freshwater fish aquaculture and seed production and farming of brackishwater shrimp. In the past, the fry and fingerlings of Indian major carp, the traditional farmed species, were captured by collectors from specific pockets in riverine breeding grounds and then transported to pond farmers by middlemen. The mode of transportation was either by boat or by fish vendor. The boats had a fish hold in the bottom with a mesh-covered hole that facilitated water exchange. The vendors carried fingerlings in clay or aluminum containers and aerated these by continuously agitating the water by hand. The former method resulted in less mortality than the latter.

Nowadays, in-country transport of live fish or spawn is generally done with oxygenated water in polythene bags. Mortalities are insignificant. Live carp and catfish broodstock are transported from one area to another by truck in aerated tanks. There is no published data on the annual volume of broodstock transfers and their economic value.

Carp seed in Bangladesh are produced by 274 hatcheries, 16 of which are run by the Department of Fisheries (DoF), three by the Fisheries Research Institute (FRI) and the rest (256) by private businesses. Present hatchery egg production stands at around 5,000 kg per annum. One kg usually contains about 0.35 to 0.5 million fertilized eggs. In general, eggs are transferred from hatcheries to nurseries and reared to the fingerling stage, then they are sold throughout the country in polythene bags with oxygenated water.

No health certification or quarantine guidelines for the transfer of aquatic animals are followed inside Bangladesh. A kg of eggs costs between Tk 2000 and Tk 15000 (US$50 to $375), depending on species, season and hatchery proximity. The price of fingerlings varies from Tk 20 to Tk200 per 100 animals, depending on species and size. Hatchery produced shrimp post larvae, both freshwater and penaeid, are limited in numbers and rarely transported very far. Natural or imported shrimp post larvae are transported throughout the country in polythene bags with oxygenated water and ice. The price of transported post larvae varies widely. During 1995, the price of 100 post larvae of *P. monodon* was between Tk 100 and Tk 400 (US$ 2.5 to $10).

International trade in live shrimp and fish seed to and from Bangladesh is not well documented. Most of the imported fish come in as broodstock. Significant large-scale trade in aquatic animals started in 1995 and mostly comprised *P. monodon* nauplii and post larvae. The total number of PLs imported during 1995 numbered 50 million and probably came mostly from Thailand, India and Myanmar. The Thai PLs came through legal channels. Post larvae from India and Myanmar cross the long and porous border by land and by water without adequate control. It is therefore difficult to estimate how many shrimp came from neighboring countries.

The price of post larval penaeid shrimps landed at Dhaka airport ranges from Tk 45-50 per 100 animals. The price of imported nauplii is unknown and is considered to be a trade secret. Live turtles, tortoises and crabs exported from Bangladesh between 1993 and 1995 fetched roughly Tk 350 million per year, and export volume remained static at a level of roughly 4000 tonnes annually. It may be worth mentioning here that most of the live turtles and tortoises from Bangladesh go to India and the volume of trade mentioned indicates only those animals legally exported. It is assumed that a greater number of the animals crosses the border illegally.

Current status of aquatic animal quarantine and health certification programmes

There is a century-old act related to the import of live animals. The act is still valid in Bangladesh and makes provision for the regulation of livestock importation, but it does not cover aquatic animals. Although the act has been amended several times to keep pace with the demands of time, it has never included fish or other aquatic organisms. The act is known as the Livestock Importation Act, 1898.

In the fisheries sector of Bangladesh, there are many acts and regulations for the conservation and management of aquatic resources. These include:

- East Bengal Protection and Conservation of Fish Act, 1950.
- East Bengal Protection and Conservation of Fish (Amendment) Act, 1963.
- East Bengal Protection and Conservation of Fish (Amendment) Ordinance, 1970.
- Protection and Conservation of Fish Rules, 1985.

- Protection and Conservation of Fish Rules, 1985 (Amendment), 1987.
- Protection and Conservation of Fish Rules, 1985 (Amendment), 1988.
- Protection and Conservation of Fish (Amendment) Act, 1995.
- Marine Fisheries Ordinance, 1983.
- Tanks Improvement Act, 1939.
- Tanks Improvement (Amendment) Ordinance 1986.
- Fish and Fish Product (Inspection and Quality Control) Ordinance 1983.
- Shrimp Culture Taxation Rules, 1992.

Unfortunately, none of the acts, ordinances or rules specifies health and quarantine guidelines for the import and export of live aquatic animals to and from Bangladesh.

As previously mentioned, several species of freshwater fish have been imported to Bangladesh since the 1950's. Most of these fish were imported by the Directorate of Fisheries for research purposes, and then later used for seed production at the farmers' level. It is therefore assumed that strict rules for quarantine and health certification from the exporting countries were followed. Private traders in Bangladesh now import over 140 species of ornamental fish for the domestic aquarium market. We are unaware if the traders obtain any health certification or follow any quarantine guidelines provided by the exporting countries.

Since the 1995 viral disease outbreak in penaeid shrimp, serious objections were raised to the import of shrimp seed without proper health certification and quarantine procedures. However, due to the absence of the relevant legislation and expertise, imports continued, providing the export country had a system of health certification and quarantine. During 1995, a committee of officials from the DoF and the FRI was set up to formulate health certification and quarantine guidelines. A draft has not yet been presented to the authorities.

It is expected that any future health and quarantine guidelines for aquatic animals will include the following:

1. The Directorate of Fisheries will be responsible for approving the introduction and transfer of live aquatic animals.
2. The Ministry of Fisheries and Livestock (MoFL) may mandate a committee comprised of researchers and officials from the DoF, the FRI and the Bangladesh Fisheries Development Corporation (BFDC) to recommend

legislation/action on aquatic animal health certification and quarantine guidelines.

3. All literature and statistics relating the impact of importing and exporting aquatic animals should be brought to the attention of the Government by fisheries/aquatic health services.

4. The future health certification and quarantine guidelines for aquatic animals in Bangladesh should be based on internationally agreed standards.

5. Promotion of general awareness among importers of aquatic diseases, parasites, bacteria and viruses and the risk posed to public health when unknown species are introduced.

6. The MoFL should specify the requirements for an aquatic animal quarantine facility. The facility must be approved and gazetted before permits to import can be issued.

At present, Bangladesh has neither the expertise nor the facilities for an effective aquatic animal health certification and quarantine system, especially for situations when a quick decision on imported animals needs to be taken. Some of the facilities available for health, disease or parasitic infection studies remain confined to universities far away from ports of entry. As already mentioned, existing legislation under the Fisheries Act does not cover health and quarantine procedures for aquatic animals.

Problems caused by the introduction and transfer of aquatic organisms

Although exotic fish have been introduced to Bangladesh's inland waters for the last three or four decades, no ecological studies have been conducted to determine whether any ecological problems resulted from their introduction. The Government of Bangladesh banned the export of frog legs a few years back due to the complaints of ecologists and entomologists. The export of frog legs greatly decreased the population of large sized frogs and unwittingly increased the numbers of insects and agricultural pests.

Some fisheries scientists have concluded that some imported carps compete with indigenous species for natural foods and ecological niches. The introduction of tilapia is blamed for the reduced production of wild weed fishes.

Furthermore, tilapia have invaded coastal and brackishwater regions and are now considered a hazard to traditional and improved traditional penaeid shrimp farming. However, tilapias also provide a significant amount of much-needed animal protein for human consumption.

Ecological studies on a man-made lake in Bangladesh, covering an area of roughly 69,000 ha, showed that production of several dozen indigenous species has decreased at an alarming rate during the last ten years, due to tilapia invasion of the lake. The most disturbing fact is that production of tilapia does not cover the loss of the combined biomass of the displaced species, and the price of tilapia is far lower than the species it replaced. However, losses in the lake's total biomass production may be also due to over exploitation. Further investigation is required. The introduction of fish like silver, bighead and common carp, etc. has reportedly reduced the production of indigenous catla (*Catla catla*), rohu (*Labeo rohita*) and mrigal (*Cirrhina mrigala*). However, the introduction of grass and black carp has had a positive ecological effect. These species control aquatic weeds and snails and increase the unit area fish production of waterbodies.

The effect of the introduction of the North African catfish (*Clarias gariepinus*) on wild indigenous fauna has yet to be investigated. Culture of North African catfish in Bangladesh is gaining in popularity because of the fish's rapid growth, easy seed production, capacity to grow in crowded ponds with poor water quality and its habit of eating anything of animal origin. However, its culture is still confined to closed systems. It has yet to be determined whether imported aquatic animals pose a threat to human health. The export of some lizard skins had reportedly increased the insect and snake populations. This practice is now banned in Bangladesh. The human health and ecological threats posed by the import and export of ornamental aquarium fish has yet to be investigated. However, aquarium fish normally live under controlled conditions, except for the guppy, which was first imported during the early 1950s for academic purposes, but now lives in the drainage system of Dhaka. The guppy can survive in dirty water and eats the larvae of mosquitoes and other insects, thus helping to clean the environment.

Recommendations for strengthening national programs in aquatic animal health certification and quarantine procedures

Since Bangladesh has no health certification and quarantine guidelines, the country needs to develop a legal framework to cover these activities. An aquatic animal act will give clear instructions to the decision-maker on how to balance the risks and the benefits associated with the introduction of a new species. Therefore, the criteria for proper certification and quarantine procedure needs to be set so that the import and export of live aquatic animals can go ahead. The following elements are necessary:

1. A specialist group under the guidance of the MFL quality management to coordinate the import and export of live aquatic animals.

2. Adequate preparation, consultation and decision making prior to the import of new species and an import or export impact assessment.
3. Adequate preparation in ensuring effective disease, parasitic, bacterial or viral risk assessment to ensure sound decision making.
4. An assessment on why a particular new species needs to be introduced in Bangladesh and how suited it would be to the environment in Bangladesh.
5. Investigation is necessary on whether the new species has any biological limitations on its future distribution.
6. Specialists' expertise and advice on the risks and benefits of any proposed species introduction.
7. Scientist working with selected species in the field of aquaculture and disease can provide disease risk assessment.
8. The importer needs to supply information on the supply source and its disease status as established through disease testing and inspection.
9. Provision to collect information on aquatic animal health and disease from a prospective importing country well in advance of the actual import date.
10. Collection of current journals, bulletins and publications on health and disease of aquatic organisms from all over the world for the people engaged in health and quarantine services.
11. Overseas quarantine, testing and importation procedures as well as the Bangladeshi quarantine requirements must be followed before issuing an aquatic animal export permit.
12. Before issuing an aquatic animal import permit, there should be consultation with the overseas certifying authority.
13. Shipments of imported or exported aquatic animals should be inspected at the port of entry or departure.
14. The imported or exported stock should be counted, species verified and an assessment of health conducted.
15. The shipment water and packaging materials should be sterilized and then disposed.
16. Any questionable shipment in terms of health and disease should be destroyed immediately.

All the above-mentioned points are recognized worldwide and it is expected that the Government of Bangladesh will agree to a draft formulated by the workshop. But in Bangladesh, and probably in some other countries, knowledge of fish disease is fragmented and incomplete, disease-testing facilities are almost absent and trained manpower in the field is limited. Therefore, a code of practice or set of rules, no matter how good it is, will not work unless the trained manpower and facilities are provided.

Cambodia

M.C. Nandeesha
Partnership for Development in Kampuchea (PADEK)
PO Box 554, Phnom Penh, Cambodia

Abstract

Various species of fish have been introduced into Cambodia. There are no regulations that prohibit the introduction of exotic species. There are no facilities and no trained staff to conduct quarantine and health certification. With the growing interest in aquaculture, Cambodia has to adopt appropriate and practical steps as soon as possible to prevent the introduction of additional species without prior evaluation.

Introduction

With the end of two decades of war, Cambodia is now emerging as an important country in the region for fisheries development. Fish is reported to contribute 75% of the dietary animal protein requirement of Cambodians. Rice and fish form the staple diet of the country's population. It is gratifying to record here that after several years of continuous rice shortages, a surplus production is anticipated for 1996. It is predicted that, at the present rate of agricultural expansion, Cambodia will regain its status as a rice exporting country by the end of the century. Despite the increases in rice output, fish production per capita is declining. Aquaculture is considered the alternative route to improving fish production, compensating for recent decreases from capture fisheries. Aquaculture is relatively new to Cambodia. Traditionally, commercial culture of some native species like snakeheads (*Channa* spp.) and pangasids (*Pangasius* spp.) existed. Recently, small-scale aquaculture has gained popularity amongst farmers. Aquaculture systems existing in the country have been described in various publications (Nandeesha 1994; Tana 1995).

International and in-country trade in aquatic organisms

Capture and culture fishery production statistics are now available for 1995. In the freshwater capture fisheries sector, a production of 72,500 tonnes was reported, while in the marine sector, 30,500 tonnes were caught. From aquaculture, a total production of 9,510 tonnes was obtained. Shrimp production was reported to be 730 tonnes. Crocodile farming is an important occupation in the Northwestern Provinces and a total of 14,691 heads was produced. Most baby crocodiles are sold to Thai traders. The total revenue realized by the Government from the fisheries sector was about US$4.5 million.

Most of the inland fish production is consumed in Cambodia, while a large portion of the marine catch is exported to Thailand. Similarly, most of the shrimp production is exported to Thailand. In fact, much of the shrimp industry involves collaboration with Thai partners. Hence most shrimp culture problems in Cambodia are akin to those encountered in Thailand. During 1995, it was reported that the incidence of shrimp diseases had increased.

All four countries of the Indo-China region are linked through the Mekong River. There are strong regional trade links between the border provinces of Cambodia and its neighbors. Border trade is most significant in Svey Ring Province with Vietnam, in Battambang Province with Thailand and in Stung Treng and Rattanakri provinces with Laos.

Current status of aquatic animal quarantine and health certification programs

At present there are no facilities capable of carrying out acceptable work on aquatic animal quarantine and health certification. The knowledge and experience of Cambodian authorities on the potential risks of introducing exotic organisms is limited. There are no trained personnel to undertake regular quarantine checks. Some facilities for animal husbandry are reportedly available as are human health centers for conducting microbiological analyses. However, owing to the high demand for these limited facilities by other priority sectors, they are not available for fish health certification.

There are no established guidelines for the introduction of aquatic organisms in Cambodia. Currently, it is the Department of Fisheries, working under the Ministry of Agriculture, which provides permission for the import of live aquatic animals. There are no health and quarantine control points at the airports, seaports or land entry points. For the last month, a new quarantine health form for people entering the country has been used. However, no restrictions are imposed on bringing plants and animals into the country. Furthermore, there is little awareness of the value of having quarantine regulations.

Problems caused by the introduction and transfer of aquatic organisms

Many fish species have been introduced into Cambodia. Unfortunately, there are no official records detailing these introductions. Based on the little information available, following is a summary of such introductions. Aquaculture activities existed in the 1960's around Phnom Penh. The Chinese community reportedly roduced Chinese carps: silver carp (*Hypophthalmichthys molitrix*), bighead carp (*Aristichthys nobilis*), grass carp (*Ctenopharyngodon idella*) and common carp (*Cyprinus carpio*). Tilapia (*Oreochromis mossambicus*) was apparently cultured in ponds on rubber plantations. After liberation of the country in 1979 from the Pol Pot regime, aquaculture activity was restarted by the Vietnamese who built the Chraing Chamres Fisheries Station near Phnom Penh. Once again, Chinese carps, the Indian carp - rohu (*Labeo rohita*) and tilapia were brought into the country. After 1993, North African catfish (*Clarias gariepinus*), Nile tilapia (*Oreochromis niloticus*) and a red tilapia (Oreochromis sp.) were introduced.

Much of Cambodia is subjected to floods and there have been cases of exotic organisms escaping into natural water bodies. Though most of the existing hatcheries are protected from flooding, these protective measures are not strong enough to overcome serious inundations which have become more prevalent recently and have contributed to environmental degradation. There are reports of sightings of common carp, silver carp and, even more unusually, of rohu, in some of the major fishing centers. Since several areas in Indo-China are flood prone and all of the countries are linked by the Mekong River, there is every possibility that exotic species regularly escape into natural waters from fish farm ponds. Farmers have increasingly tried to prevent the escape of valuable stock by encircling ponds with nets, building bunds and other measures. However, these protective measures have not been completely effective in preventing the escape of exotic fish. There have also been instances of stocking natural waters with exotic species like tilapia and carps. However, as a result of improved awareness of the detrimental effects this can cause, the practice appears to have ended.

The issue of promoting aquaculture with exotic species is often questioned considering the potential danger of exotic species to the aquatic environment. However, if exotic species are not to be used in aquaculture, there are very few indigenous species appropriate for small-farm culture environment. Except silver barb and *Pangasius*, there are no other native fish which are available for aquaculture. Even among these two, silver barb is loosing the interest of farmers owing to its poor growth and farmers are not in a position to provide quality artificial food to *Pangasius* in order to obtain good growth.

Some fear that, in the lower Mekong area, the fisheries might soon be impacted by exotic species if preventative measures to stop their escape into the river are not developed and implemented now. More information is required on the positive and negative impacts of exotics. While it would be impracticable and undesirable to stop the development of exotic species aquaculture in the region, it would be appropriate to intensify research on native species and to identify those most suitable for culture. Existing fish and shrimp disease problems show that it is easy for diseases which are prevalent in other Indo-

Chinese nations to infect Cambodia too. With the establishment of national hatcheries, trade in fish seed from neighboring countries is gradually being reduced.

Recommendations for strengthening national programs in aquatic animal health certification and quarantine procedures

The Ministry of the Environment is currently being strengthened and has decided to put biodiversity programs high on the agenda. However, there is still no clear legislation preventing the introduction of exotic organisms. It is necessary for the country to introduce such legislation sooner rather than later.

Human resources are a major constraint. There are no adequately trained personnel to undertake fish disease or quarantine work. It has been suggested that high priority be given to setting up fish disease facilities. At the moment, the Royal Agricultural University cannot improve the quality of education it offers because its infrastructure is so limited. It is necessary to draw up practical plans and implement these in order to develop infrastructure and human resources. Most importantly, there is a need to develop understanding amongst the countries of the Mekong region on trade in aquatic animals and the importance of following quarantine procedures at all entry points. Discussion on preventing the escape into natural waters of exotic species especially in flood prone areas would also be very useful.

Conclusion

Promoting an idealistic approach on the introduction of exotic organisms may not be a practicable idea. However, it should still be a priority to increase people's awareness on the procedures to be adopted for the introduction of exotic species. Careful evaluation and introduction protect biodiversity and contribute to food productivity.

References

Nandeesha, M.C. (1994). Aquaculture in Cambodia. INFOFISH International, (2): 42-48.

Tana, T.S. (1995). Cambodia, p 83-89. Report on a Regional Study on the Environmental Assessment and Management of Aquaculture Development. FAO/NACA, Bangkok, Thailand.

People's Republic of China

Cen Feng

National Fishery Technology Extension Centre
Ministry of Agriculture
People's Republic of China

Abstract

The annual yield of aquatic products steadily increased in China from 1990 to 1994. In 1994 aquaculture products accounted for 53% of the country's total fishery production. China has existing legislation which covers some aspects of health certification and quarantine procedures of aquatic organisms, but it is incomplete. Further research is needed to understand the ecological effects of new aquatic species introductions. International cooperation will go a long way to establishing common guidelines on health certification and quarantine of aquatic animals.

Introduction

China's fisheries industry has developed rapidly during the 1990s. The annual yield of aquatic products reached 12.37 million tonnes in 1990, and increased to 21.46 million tonnes in 1994. Aquaculture has achieved remarkable development; its proportion of total fishery production increased from 49% (6.08 million tonnes) in 1990 to 53% (11.35 million tonnes) in 1994. The annual rate of increase between 1991 and 1994 was 16.9% higher than that of 1986 to 1990 when it was 14.5%. The development speed is closely related to the strengthening of health management of aquaculture in China.

International and in-country trade in aquatic organisms

In China, most aquatic products are traded in domestic markets. People in the coastal areas and in the inland cities consume aquatic products. Domestic trade accounts for more than 90% of total trade which involves transporting and marketing fresh and frozen fish, shrimps, processed products and both adult and larval organisms used in aquaculture.

In 1994, the total export volume was 684,000 tonnes with a total value of US$2.6 billion, most of which was frozen fish, shrimps, processed products and a small amount of living aquatic organisms. Just less than 100,000 tonnes of living aquatic organisms were exported and about 1,000 tonnes were imported during the same year.

Current status of aquatic animal quarantine and health certification programmes

A system of aquatic animal health quarantine and health certification has never been implemented for internal transport and marketing of aquatic products (including living organisms). The quality of aquatic products which are put on the domestic market must conform to food sanitation standards. Export products must meet the criteria of the "Export Standard of Aquatic Products", as well as any demands expressed by the import country.

The Chinese government attaches great importance to health management and quarantine of aquatic organisms. The principal laws and regulations that have been drafted and enacted are the People's Republic of China Quarantine Law for the Import and Export of Animals and Plants, the Detailed Rules, and The Quarantine Order of Imported Finfish and Shrimp.

As aquaculture diseases are spreading in China, a National Aquaculture Disease Control Meeting was held by the Ministry of Agriculture in Beijing in November 1995. The meeting pointed out that legislation is a focal point in the management of larvae, feed, medicine and water used in aquaculture and that it should be strengthened. It is planned to put the health license procedure for hatcheries into practice step by step.

At present, the Animal and Plant General Quarantine Institute, which works under the Ministry of Agriculture, is in charge of quarantine procedures in China. The Institute has offices at each port of entry and is responsible for carrying out the work. Until the early 1990s, China had 46 quarantine institute offices at sea ports, airports and at inland borders and nearly 70 sub-branches. In addition, there are 30 port animal and plant quarantine stations in provincial capitals. Some of the stations also have animal and plant isolation areas.

Most of the quarantine experts are concentrated on the animal and plant quarantine system, and those doing aquatic organisms disease research are in the fisheries institutes or some oceanic institutes. The Bureau of Fisheries under the Ministry of Agriculture is responsible for the approval for introducing new species from abroad, drawing up aquaculture research programs and making assessments of results.

Problems caused by the introduction and transfer of aquatic organisms

By the early 1990s, China had introduced 60 exotic species from abroad. Some exotic species, such as the Atlantic bay scallop (*Agropecten irradians*), the rainbow trout (*Oncorhynchus mykiss*), the Nile tilapia (*Oreochromis niloticus*) and the pirapatinga or freshwater pomano (*Piaractus brachypomus*), have been developed on a commercial scale in China, bringing economic benefits. However, the ecological impacts of such introductions have not yet been studied in-depth. Currently the main problems are as follows:

- The appearance of new disease pathogens when exotic species are introduced. In the 1980's, IPN (Infectious Haematopoietic Necrosis) virus was introduced with rainbow trout eggs. The Chinese rainbow trout industry was seriously affected. MBV (Monodon baculovirus) has often been recorded as a result of introducing adult shrimp (*Penaeus monodon*).

- Controls on movement of aquatic animals under the quarantine system have not yet been established. It is difficult to control disease under such circumstances.

Little is known about human health problems caused by the movement of aquatic organisms. Nevertheless, the outbreak of infective hepatitis in Shanghai, which then spread elsewhere in China, was related to harvesting of the mollusc arca (*Scapharca subcrenata*) from polluted coastal waters and transporting them in unsanitary conditions.

Recommendations for strengthening national programs in aquatic animal health certification and quarantine procedures

The Chinese Government takes great interest in its national program for the health certification and quarantine of aquatic organisms. It is hoped that the following work will be carried out:

- Establishment of international conventions or agreements. There should be prohibitions on aquatic organisms moving from diseased areas. During normal trade, the export country should provide health certification that the import country should double check.

- Agreement on common diagnostic/detection methods and forecast technologies for dangerous pathogens.

- Establishment of a regional disease information network to regularly report on disease occurrence and spread, control methods, *etc.*

- Establishment of an international clearinghouse comprised of experts to facilitate technology exchange and cooperation.

India

Punyabrata Das
National Bureau of Fish Genetic Resources
351/28 Dariapur, Talkatora Road
Lucknow-226004
India

Abstract

India has an aquatic animal export business. It also imports some species. Like most Asian countries, it faces the growing problem of new pathogens being introduced with the import of exotic species. In some cases, introduced pathogens have damaged valuable fish and shrimp stocks. Some legislation relating to the import and export of live, aquatic animals does exist, but it is not complete. Similarly, there is good expertise and some well-equipped facilities for fish disease diagnosis and disease prevention, however, they are not adequate for health certification and quarantine procedures. Changes in Government responsibilities mean that the National Bureau for Fish Genetic Resources has been mandated to take on this type of work. It is now time to develop the relevant national legislation on aquatic animal health certification and quarantine and to ensure that the necessary manpower and facilities are provided to implement them.

Introduction

The rapid globalization of the fish trade and the increasing demand for exotic species of fish, crustaceans, molluscs and other groups of aquatic animals has resulted in the unwitting dissemination of pathogens and microbes from one country to another. Most Asian countries, including India, face the problem of new diseases due to new pathogens of foreign origin being introduced with aquatic animal species. These pathogens have, in some cases, damaged valuable domestic fish and shrimp stocks.

Since the exchange of aquatic organisms between countries has many advantages, it is necessary to follow quarantine procedures to ensure that pathogens do not accompany them. Efforts to prevent the spread of exotic diseases of aquatic animals generally follows three strategies: farm certification, shipment inspection, and quarantine. The basic aim of quarantine is to minimize the risk of spreading exotic pests and pathogens into new geographical areas. A detailed quarantine infrastructure is thus indispensable if the risks associated with expanded exchange of germplasm material are to be effectively controlled

International and in-country trade in aquatic organisms

India is fortunate to be endowed with plenty of excellent ornamental aquatic species, including about 50 types of fish, many molluscs, plants, echinoderms, coelenterates, *etc.*, and many of these are attractive to foreign markets. Indian carps in particular perform well in freshwater aquaculture systems, yielding good economic returns. Thus, there exists a worldwide market for Indian ornamental fish and possibly a South and Southeast Asian market for carp seed.

The international trade also includes the import of ornamental fish for aquaria. There are some 100 species of fish that have been brought into India. About a half a dozen of these are food fish and a few others are larvicidal fish that have a useful purpose; the rest are ornamental fish. While the quantity of live aquatic animals imported into India remains small, the amount exported is substantial, as Table 1 indicates.

Exports of live aquatic animals include ornamental and other fish, lobsters, shrimp and crabs and are given in Table 2. Table 3 lists the infrastructural facilities available for marine product preparation in India. With our modern, intensive aquaculture industry and high yielding production technology, there is an increasing demand for Indian major carps, Chinese carps and shrimp seed. Until recently, the center for carp seed production was West Bengal, from where it was transported to the rest of the country. More recently, other states have been producing seed, but West Bengal remains the principal producer maintaining trade with the rest of the country. In 1993-94, West Bengal produced 7,540 million fry. The World Bank-assisted seed production plan, now in its 5th five-year cycle, was lodged with the Fisheries Corporations of different states, who supply seed to the growers within those states. In addition, there are private seed producers who supply state production centers. Table 4 shows freshwater fish seed production from 1973 to 1993.

Similarly, there is a regular movement of shrimp seed from collection points and hatcheries, both private and public, to other maritime states where they are ongrown. Trade in freshwater prawn, *Macrobrachium rosenbergii*, seed also exists. Frozen shrimp is an important earner of foreign exchange.

The principal countries importing marine fish products from India include Japan, U.S.A., Spain, France, Singapore, Taiwan, Hong Kong, Greece, U.K., Belgium, Netherlands, Thailand and countries in the Middle East.

Calcutta fish market, the largest in the country, receives fish from both neighboring and very distant states. Similarly, markets in other cosmopolitan cities like Delhi, Madras, Bombay and Bangalore receive fish supplies from the neighboring states. In 1992, the total quantity of fish marketed in India as fresh was 4.4 million tonnes. In 1994 that figure was 4.6 million tonnes.

Other species traded in-country include: ornamental fish, mussels, tortoises, echinoderms and coelenterates.

Current status of aquatic animal quarantine and health certification programs

The decision-making procedures for importing and exporting aquatic animals vary somewhat. These are described below.

- ***Import***

Anyone wishing to import an exotic species for aquaculture or ornamental purposes must submit an application stating the name of the fish, the country of origin and other details to the Fisheries Development Commissioner in the Union Ministry of Agriculture. On receipt of the application, the proposal is passed to the National Committee for Introduction of Exotic Aquatic Species of the Indian Council of Agricultural Research (ICAR) for scientific comment and a recommendation. The committee, chaired by the Director of the National Bureau of Fish Genetic Resources, and comprised of other expert senior scientific personnel, studies the animal's biology, genetics, habitat, *etc* from available literature and then compares this information with any similar species indigenous to India. The committee also considers whether the animal in question would compete with any existing species or cause damage to the ecosystem if it were to escape into natural waters.

It is important that any new species contributes to enhancing production, but at the same time has no negative influence on biodiversity. A consensus decision based on all of these aspects is taken and the recommendation is passed from the ICAR to the Union Ministry of Agriculture which, in turn, communicates it to the applicant. When agreement is given to import an exotic species, it is held on a farm for observation and its health is checked. If it is carrying any pathogens or disease, the entire stock is destroyed.

- ***Export***

Live aquatic animals exported from India are usually for research or commercial purposes. If animals are to be used for research purposes, then the following procedure, still being finalized, is followed. On receipt of an application, the Union Ministry of Agriculture or the Ministry of the Environment and Forest, passes it to a nodal institution for their recommendation. The nodal body for marine aquatics is the Central Marine Fisheries Research Institute (CMFRI). For freshwater aquatic animals it is the National Bureau of Fish Genetic Resources (NBFGR). Any additional assistance can be requested from the other ICAR institutes and State Agricultural Universities.

The nodal organization always considers whether or not the animal is purely for research purposes. Transfer of stock for breeding or for the development of new varieties is not normally permitted. Trade in rare, vulnerable or endangered species is never permitted. The recommendations of the nodal body would then be passed on to the Ministry, who either approves or rejects the application. If successful, the germplasm is then supplied under the provisions of a Material Transfer Agreement.

Export for commercial purposes is currently regulated by the Union Ministry of Commerce under the export-import policy of the Foreign Trade Act (1992) and its subsequent amendments which deal with fish products. Marine aquarium fish for export are examined by the Wildlife Authorities in Calcutta to check whether they are endangered. If so, export is prohibited.

The list of species prohibited for export does not contain the names of any fish genetic resources. The list needs to be revised to protect all living, rare, vulnerable and endangered aquatic animals.

Whenever any living aquatic animal is exported, a pathologist must certify its health and only then will customs clear the consignment.

- The National Bureau mandated to recommend legislation for introduction of new species.

While ecosystem-based research institutes do exist in India and they do contribute to policy making, it is the National Bureau of Fish Genetic Resources (NBFGR) which is mandated to recommend legislation on introducing new species. All activities concerning quarantine will soon be assumed by the NBFGR as soon as it acquires the necessary infrastructure and manpower. Work in this direction is currently in progress. It is planned that similar facilities will also be developed in the regional centers of the NBFGR (northern, southern and eastern India).

- Existing facilities and expertise available for aquatic animal health certification and quarantine

There are fish pathology divisions at the various fishery institutions around the country. A similar facility will be established at the National Bureau of Fish Genetic Resources in the near future. Expertise on aquatic animal disease diagnosis, and prophylactic and therapeutic measures already exists in India.

Health certification would be conducted through farm studies and laboratory investigations at quarantine centers. Such centers do not presently exist. Though some facilities at certain institutions could be used for health certification, proper farm facilities are yet to be developed, although one is planned for the National Bureau of Fish Genetic Resources.

- Existing legislation

No detailed legislation for aquatic animal quarantine or health certification exists as of yet. The current regulations solely call for the applicant to obtain an import or export permit. These rules stipulate that an export permit request will be rejected for aquatic species with any disease, some marine shells and seaweeds (except agarophytes in a processed form). So India still needs to enact specific legislation in this area.

Problems caused by the introduction and transfer of aquatic organisms

- Ecological imbalance caused by introductions and transfers

In India, the introduction of exotic fish has had a mixed reaction. Some exotics, like trout (*Salmo trutta*, *Oncorhynchus mykiss*), have filled a vacant niche with no competition from any native species. Others, like grass carp *(Ctenopharyngodon idella*), silver carp (*Hypophthalmichthys molitrix*) and the common carp (*Cyprinus* carpio) have helped boost freshwater aquaculture production, but in some cases have negatively impacted native fish.

Silver carp was introduced in 1971-72 in the multipurpose Gobindsagar Reservoir (H.P.). Its arrival has resulted into a sharp decline of the dominant native species *Catla catla* due to overlapping feeding habits and habitat. Silver carp production in the reservoir increased from 0.60 tonnes to 334 tonnes in 10 years (from 1977-78 to 1987-88), while *Catla catla* production, which was 210 tonnes in 1977-78, declined to 36.7 tonnes in 1987-88.

Similarly, in Kalgarhi Reservoir (M.P.) the catla population has declined as a result of competition with silver carp.

Common carp was introduced in different lakes of Kashmir and Manipur and *Cirrhina* species in Krishnaraj Sagar and Gilna reservoirs. This resulted in a sharp decline of *Schizothorax* spp. in the same places.

Mossambique tilapia, *Oreochromis mossambicus*, has had a negative impact on indigenous species. In Amaravati and Vaigai reservoirs and Powai and Jaisawand lakes it has eliminated almost all other species, including the major carps and the indigenous catfish, because of its prolific breeding habits and omnivorous feeding behavior.

Gambusia affinis has practically ousted all other indigenous species in Ooty Lake in Tamil Nadu, damaging the economy of the lake area.

- Parasites and disease introduced

In spite of prohibiting the import of fish seed during the past few years, the aquaculture industry in India has suffered some serious setbacks. From 1988 to 1992, there was an outbreak of Epizootic Ulcerative Syndrome (EUS) in the north east of the country that gradually spread to the north. During 1994, lymphoid organ necrosis (similar to yellowhead disease in Thailand) appeared in tiger shrimp, *Penaeus monodon,* farms. Infections of haematopoietic hypodermal necrosis virus and white spot syndrome were a problem in *P. indicus* in Andhra Pradesh. Several other new diseases have also occurred in penaeid farms in Balsad (Gujrat), Bombay (Maharashtra) and other states. These were not seen in the country before and may have been exotic introductions. Further investigation may reveal their origin. Antibiotic and herbal medicines have had some success against shrimp diseases.

No information was available on any human health problems and zoonoses stemming from movement of aquatic organisms.

Recommendations for strengthening national programs in aquatic animal health certification and quarantine procedures

- Legislative requirements

It is necessary to enact the appropriate legislation for aquatic animal health and quarantine procedures in India. The legislation should, amongst other things, stipulate the following:

1. a quarantine system must be made compulsory;
2. the import and export of aquatic organisms requires a permit from the Government of India;
3. import and export should be limited to one or two designated ports;
4. health certification from the exporting country is a pre-requisite;
5. all organisms meant for import and export should be kept in a quarantine center for observation for an appropriate period of time;
6. imported water and any accompanying parasites must be safely disposed;
7. a well-equipped laboratory and farm facility are essential for quarantine work. This is in addition to existing facilities at different labs;
8. a complete list of aquatic animals prohibited from export needs to be prepared;
9. rare, vulnerable or endangered species must not be exported;
10. breeding stock and stock developed for new varieties should not be exported; and
11. imposition of penalties for non-compliance of quarantine and health certification rules.

- Infrastructure and human resource development

Well-equipped laboratory and farm facilities for quarantine are not yet available in India. A separate quarantine research laboratory building with equipment for diagnosis of aquatic animal diseases is necessary. Equally important is a well laid-out fish farm for field studies on exotic species. NBFGR, in the course of time, should develop this priority infrastructure.

- Human resource development

The human resources for a quarantine center should be coordinated through initial recruitment of qualified staff. Their training should be updated both within the country and abroad to ensure that the quality of their work remains accurate and professional.

In view of the usual constraints in a developing county, NACA/FAO collaboration and assistance in both infrastructure and human resource development would be welcome.

- Requirements and interest in a regional program to meet national needs

In view of the present situation, we are interested in strengthening our national capabilities with the addition of organized quarantine centers, more technical know-how and skilled personnel. India also encourages regional collaborative programs, especially as we share many common aquatic resources in the region. We would highly welcome international programs on this subject and remain interested in any NACA/FAO initiatives.

Table 1: Export of live aquatic animals from India

Year	**Export**	
	Quantity (mt)	Value (million Rupees*)
1991-92	595	19.8
1992-93	573	34.9
1993-94	744	67.1

1 US$ = 35.7 Rupees (September 1997)

Table 2: Marine product exports by category

Items	1991-1992		1992-1993		1993-1994	
	Q	V	Q	V	Q	V
Frozen shrimp	76,151	9,791.2	74,393	11,803	86,541	17,707.3
Frozen fish	49,333	1,432.0	75,376	2,324	94,002	2,960
Frozen squids	25,529	1,093.8	30,364	1,519	34,741	1,924.7
Frozen cuttlefish	12,437	609.1	18,981	11,88.8	18,998	1,381.8
Frozen lobster tails	1,628	553.0	1,613	433.4	1,455	426.8
Dried items	2,195	31.4	3,357	50.1	2,602	162.7
Live items	595	19.8	573	34.9	744	67.1
Misc.items	3,954	228.6	3,945	321.4	4,857	405.8
Total	171.822	13,758.9	20.951.2	176.74.6	243,940	25,036.2

Q: quantity in tonnes; V: value in million Rupees

Table 3: Infrastructural facilities available for marine product preparation.

Facilities	Number of plants	Capacity (tonnes/day)
Freezing	308	4,013.75
Canning	23	81.50
Ice making	133	2,034.00
Fish meal	18	333.50
Cold storage	380	62,170.00
Peeling sheds	880	2,268.55

Table 4: Fish seed production in India

Year	Fish seed production (in million fry)
1973-74	409.0
1978-79	912.0
1984-85	5,639.0
1985-86	6,322.0
1986-87	7,601.0
1987-88	8,608.0
1988-89	9,325.40
1989-90	9,691.16
1990-91	10,332.0
1991-92	12,491.0

Indonesia

Hariyadi Mangunwiryo

Central Research Institute for Fisheries
Slipi, Jakarta,
Indonesia

Abstract

Indonesia operates successful capture and culture fisheries sectors. As trade in live aquatic organisms increases, so too do the concerns over the introduction of harmful pathogens and diseases. Many of the most dangerous pathogens and diseases in the aquaculture industry do not exist in Indonesia. The country is aware of the need for an effective quarantine program for aquatic animals and has already initiated actions to strengthen the existing system.

Introduction

Indonesia, an ASEAN member state, consists of 17,000 islands, straddling the equator between 6°N to 11°S latitude. The country is endowed with rich natural resources that include numerous kinds of animals, plants and fish - all of which need to be protected and conserved. These biotic natural resources constitute a basic capital of the country and they ought to be taken into account when planning national development. Such development has as its objective the realization of a just and prosperous society based on the ideology of Pancasila (the five principles) and the 1945 Constitution.

The country is also endowed with intensive marine waters consisting of 3.1 million km^2 of territorial waters and 2.7 million km^2 of exclusive economic zone (EEZ). Indonesian marine fisheries potential is very large - up to 6.7 million tonnes per year. At the same time freshwater fisheries have been reported as under-utilized (CRIFI, 1995).

Aquaculture in Indonesia has developed rapidly both in traditional and more modern intensive systems. The total potential area for aquaculture development is estimated to be about 1,313,400 ha, consisting of about 840,000 ha of coastal area for brackishwater ponds (tambak), 470,000 ha of inland waters, of which 180,000 ha could be developed for freshwater ponds, 155,000 ha for rice fish culture and 135,000 ha for pen or cage culture. In addition, there are about 86,000 ha of marine areas for seafarming development, comprising 3,500 ha for finfish, 57,000 ha for shellfish, 23,000 ha for seaweed and 2,500 ha for sea cucumber or mollusc culture (Adisukresno, 1992). Freshwater fisheries potential is estimated to be about 800,000 to 900,000 tonnes per year, but only 40% of this is realized. Several marine fisheries commodities from Indonesia, including tuna, shrimp, squid and pearl oyster, have been successfully exported (CRIFI, 1995).

As a national program, the development of Indonesian fisheries has been directed towards:

1. Improving the income and welfare of fishermen and fish farmers by increasing fisheries production, in both quality and quantity, in order to satisfy food and nutrient requirements.
2. Fulfilling national industrial raw material requirements and to raise the added value of fisheries products.
3. Increasing foreign exchange from fisheries exports.
4. Increasing the awareness of sustainable resources and production methodologies.

The shift of fisheries production structure from 90% capture and 10% culture to 84.5% capture and 15.5% culture is promising, as this shows that fisheries is trying to follow the principle of sustainable utilization and management of natural resources.

The total fish production has increased from 1,647,665 tonnes with a value of Rp. 378,851 million in 1978 to over 2,670,000 tonnes with a value of Rp. 616,014 million in 1987, while foreign exchange earnings during the same period also increased from US$193,424,000 to US$712,199,000. Shrimp has consistently contributed the largest amount to Indonesian fisheries exports, at 30% in volume and 80% in value terms. The decline in capture shrimp fishing due to the ban of trawlers in 1980 coupled with the increasing pressure on certain fishing areas, has made the government attach high priority to shrimp culture development (Adisukresno, 1992).

International and in-country trade in aquatic organisms

Data from 1993 show that the export of live-fish is increasing from year to year, along with the effort to increase the fishery production and fulfill export requirements. The live fish export has increased from 27,964,216 fish in 1988/1989 to 37,364,070 fish in 1991/1992, whereas fry seed exports have decreased from 31,270,000 fish to only 3,138,460 fish (CAQ, 1993). Another report described fisheries exports as reaching 421,000 tonnes with a value of US$ 1.26 billion in 1992 (CRIFI, 1995). The most serious matter affecting the import of live fish into Indonesia is the attempt to bring in new species with aquaculture potential. Examples of this are: *Anguilla* sp. from Europe, *Oreochromis niloticus* from the U.S.A. and koi carp (*Cyprinus carpio*)from Japan.

The import of live fish has increased from 65,834 fish in 1988/1989 to 157,870 fish in 1991/1992. There was no import of fry/seed in 1988/1989, but by 1991/1992 the number had risen to 13,028 fry/seed. During the same period, domestic live fish traffic decreased from 72,104,526 fish in 1988/1989 to

8,578,427 fish in 1991/1992, although that situation has probably reversed since 1992(more recent data were not available).

Indonesia has imported species from countries where epizootics, unheard of here, have already occurred i.e. Japan, America, Europe, *etc.* The ever increasing international and inter-island movement of fish enhances the likelihood of introducing and disseminating aquatic animal pathogens and diseases that may damage Indonesia's biotic natural resources (Davy and Chouinard, 1982; CAQ, 1995).

Current status of aquatic animal quarantine and health certification programs

Considering that most serious aquatic animal pathogens have not yet been detected in the Indonesian Archipelago and that the few which do exist here are confined to certain islands, most of the country needs to be protected as "disease free zones" by strong national legislation. Furthermore, the existing colonial laws regarding animal, plant and fish quarantine can no longer keep up with developments and the national interest. They should therefore be replaced. As they stand, animal, fish and plant quarantine is not adequately covered. New provisions must be drawn up and enacted as laws.

In 1992, Law no.16 concerning animal, fish and plant quarantine was endorsed by Parliament. It will assist the quarantine service, providing a basis for enforcement. Species covered by Law no.16, 1992 include:

- Finfish (Pisces).
- Shrimp, crabs and allied species (Crustacea).
- Shell-fish, cuttlefish, octopus, snails and allied species (Mollusca).
- Sea-cucumbers, sea-urchins and allied species (Echinodermata).
- Frogs, and allied species (Amphibia).
- Crocodiles, turtles, tortoises, lizards, water snakes and allied species (Reptilia).
- Whales, dolphins, sea-cows and allied species (Mammalia).
- Sea-weeds and other aquatic plants (algae).
- Other aquatic biota related to the above - mentioned species and preserved fish.
- Organization of fish quarantine systems.

In Indonesia, agricultural quarantine consists of animal, plant and fish quarantine under the direct responsibility of the Centre for Agricultural

Quarantine (CAQ) (Indonesian abbreviation "PUSKARA") supervised by the Ministry of Agriculture. CAQ is directly responsible to the Minister of Agriculture.

The Minister of Agriculture Decree No.519/Kpts/OT.210/VIII/1988, established the Regional Office of the Fish Quarantine Service (FQS), in Jakarta, which has five suboffices or Fish Quarantine Stations in Medan, Jakarta, Surabaya, Denpasar and Ujung Pandang consisting of 25 working areas at airports and seaports all over the country.

From 1994 until now, based on Minister of Agriculture Decree No.800/Kpts/OT.210/12/94, issued on 13 December 1994, four kinds of Fish Quarantine Service (FQS) have been set up as follows:

- Two Fish Quarantine Services in Jakarta and Ujung Pandang (the largest of which also acts as a reference laboratory).
- Seven FQS stations in: Medan, Palembang, Surabaya, Ngurah Rai, Mataram, Balikpapan and Jayapura.
- Five FQS posts in: Padang, Banjarbaru, Pontianak, Menado and Kendari.
- Working areas in all airports/seaports.

Each kind of service has self-autonomy and is directly responsible to the Director/Head of Centre for Agricultural Quarantine (CAQ) in Jakarta.

- Import requirements

According to Minister of Agriculture Decree No.169/Kpts/Lb.730/3/1990, places of entry for import are: the airport of Sukarno-Hatta (Jakarta), at Regional Quarantine Service, Polonia Airport (Medan, at Fish Quarantine Station), Ngurah Rai Airport (Bali, at Fish Quarantine Station) and Biak Airport (Irian Jaya, at Fish Quarantine Station). Fish importations must be accompanied by a Health Certificate from the country of origin giving details of the fish or parts of fish in transit (but not the media/carrier, which is classified as "other articles" e.g., water, packaging, other biological products, fish feed, cultures and other growing media).

- Export requirements

Based on Minister Agriculture Decree No.245/Kpts/ LB.730/ 4/1990 places of export include: the airport of Polonia, Blang Bintang, Simpang Tiga, Tabing, Hang Nadim, Sultan Mahmud Badarudin II, Sukarno - Hatta (Jakarta), Juanda (Surabaya), Supadio, Sepinggan, Tarakan, Ngurah Rai (Bali), Hasanudin (Ujung Pandang), Sam Ratulangi (Manado), Sentani and Biak (Irian Jaya).

- Prohibitions on import and export of certain fish species

Based on Minister of Agriculture Decree No. 179/Kpts/Um/ 3/1982, the importation of certain live fish species, including piranha (*Serrasalmus* sp.), vampire catfish (*Vandelia* sp), alligator gar (*Lepisosteus* sp.), *Silurus alapis*, *Esox masquinongy*, electric eel (*Electrophorus electricus*) and *Tetraodon* spp. is prohibited. These species are dangerous not only to human life but also to fishery resources. If they are found during quarantine inspection, they have to be destroyed unless they are for research/scientific purposes or for something special like a zoo collection, in which case they reauire the appropriate permit from the Minister of Agriculture.

Legislation contained in Minister of Agriculture Decree no. 700/Kpts/IK-120/10/1989 describes the prohibition on exporting penaeid shrimp including *Penaeus monodon*, *P. japonicus* and *P. merguiensis*, over the size of 20 cm. The objective of this regulation is to protect shrimp resources from unlimited exploitation.

Other regulations contained in Minister of Agriculture Decree no. 214/Kpts/Um/1973 prohibit the export of: *Anguilla* spp. fry less than 5 mm in diameter; *Botia macracanthus* larger than 15 cm; and *Macrobrachium rosenbergii* larger than 8 cm. Finally, Minister of Agriculture Decree No. 382/Kpts/IK-120/6/1987 prohibits the export of *Chanos chanos* fry from Java and Madura, Lampung, South Kalimantan, East Kalimantan, South Sulawesi and South eastern Sulawesi.

Health Certificates issued by the Centre for Agricultural Quarantine, Ministry of Agriculture, come in several formats. The export form asks for: a description on the consignment and a sanitary declaration.

- Additional information.

The health certificate for domestic fish (within Indonesian territory) consists of:

- Fish names (common and scientific).
- Quantity.
- Name and address of sender.
- Name and address of receiver.
- Area or port of destination.
- Date of shipment/transfer.
- Date of quarantine action/implementation.
- Means of transportation.

- Other documents.
- Objective of shipment/transfer.

The certificate for Fish Quarantine Release consists of:

- Fish names (general and scientific)
- Quantity.
- Name of owner.
- Address of origin.
- Country of shipment.
- Means of transportation.
- Other documents.
- Objective of shipments/transfer.

In general, quarantine action conducted by officials includes inspection, isolation, observation, treatment, detention, refusal, destruction and release (especially for imports and domestic fish traffic).

Problems caused by the introduction and transfer of aquatic organisms

- Ecological problems

In Indonesia, studies have been undertaken to investigate links between disease occurrence, water quality/pollution and host susceptibility, although understanding of the virulence/pathogenicity and serotypes of pathogens from disease outbreaks, role of water quality changes and host susceptibility is still limited. This limitation is due to the lack of advanced laboratory techniques, expertise and facilities.

Water pollution arising from freshwater fish farms, including cage culture and running water tank systems, has caused some deterioration of water quality in parts of west Java, which has contributed to serious outbreaks of fish diseases (Adisukresno, 1992). Parasitic diseases on carp farms are reportedly more severe during periods of heavy rainfall as a result of run-off of organic matter from surrounding agricultural lands. There have been some very severe mortalities of common carp in cage farms in Saguling and other reservoirs as a result of "upwelling" of water which is low in oxygen and high in hydrogen sulfide and ammonia. Reported losses are up to 40 tonnes from over 1300 cages (Adisukresno, 1992), and a severe fishkill causing thousands of dead fish was also reported from the same reservoir in 1995.

The government of Indonesia is also concerned about the environmental impact of shrimp culture, particularly the impact on mangrove resources and water quality. In Java and Sumatra there have been problems with too many farms in relation to the available water supply and ability of the environment to disperse pond effluent. This overcrowding problem can also be linked to outbreaks of shrimp disease. New regulations have been introduced which require environmental impact assessments to be carried out for proposed shrimp farms in an attempt to avoid or to reduce such problems.

Little information is available on disease and environmental impacts in marine fish culture, although outbreaks of vibriosis may be linked to poor water quality at cage culture sites. Some studies indicate that, especially in nearshore coastal waters, water pollution is the most significant contributor to fish losses through disease (infectious/non-infectious causes). The government is taking some measures to identify the sources of coastal pollution and implement pollution control measures (e.g., water treatment of land-based discharges (Taufik, 1995)).

Further studies are urgently needed concerning the relationship between water quality, host susceptibility and the biology or pathogenicity of pathogens. Information derived from such studies would help in selecting the most important pathogens for quarantine purposes (Cholik, 1992; Haryani, 1995).

The large size and different ecological zones in Indonesia mean that introduction of exotic species and aquatic animal pathogens can be considered as potentially significant, both within Indonesia as well as in relation to other countries. At least 22 exotic aquatic species have been introduced into Indonesia either as ornamental fish and plants or for culture purposes or accidentally with other organisms (e.g., the mollusc *Anodonta woodiana*) (Adisukresno, 1992). Environmental impacts of such introductions are uncertain, although some have had very significant impacts (e.g., the water hyacinth). The import of diseased fish was also implicated in the severe outbreak of ulcerative fish disease which affected common carp in the early 1980s, a problem which forced the Government of Indonesia to consider strengthening quarantine systems for aquatic animals.

Epizootic ulcerative syndrome (EUS) is considered the most important disease in freshwater fish since its outbreak in 1980s (Rukyani, 1993). The disease still causes mortality in both cultured and wild species, such as catfishes, jelawat, snakehead, gouramy and common carp. The economic loss due to the outbreak of EUS has been reported at about US$ 2 million per year (Rukyani, 1993). Recent studies suggest that the fungus *Aphanomyces* causes EUS (ACIAR Project, 1992; cited by Rukyani, 1993). Other disease problems in freshwater fish culture include the bacterial diseases vibriosis and hemorrhagic septicemia and parasitic diseases caused by *Myxobolus*, *Trichodina*, *Lernaea*, *Gyrodactylus*, *Dactylogyrus* and *Ichthyophthirius*.

Penaeid shrimp in Indonesia have also been affected by viral pathogens causing mortalities in shrimp culture. Monodon baculovirus (MBV) was reported in 1987 (Rukyani, 1993), since which time it is commonly blamed as a major cause of shrimp mortality. Whether or not MBV is the primary cause of mortalities remains to be seen, particularly as a high incidence of MBV infection is commonly associated with poor water quality management and/or water pollution (e.g., self pollution from pond effluent, domestic or industrial pollution). Other viral diseases have also been reported (clinically and histopathologically), but no clear information on the damage/mortality caused by shrimp viruses is available. Yellowhead virus (YHV) caused by baculovirus has recently been suspected in Indonesia.

Since June/July 1993, large numbers of grouper had been dying in sea cages in northern Sumatra, due to so-called "sleepy grouper disease." The outbreak in Sumatra may be due to a viral pathogen, which is new to Indonesia, but more diagnostic work is required. Whilst the epidemiology and some histopathology suggested the presence of an iridovirus, electron microscopy and immuno/histopathological studies failed to confirm the diagnosis. The term "golden eye disease" (GED) has also been used for this disease, as it describes a fatal clinical sign of *Epinephelus tauvina* (Owens, 1994). Subsequent work on viral confirmation is underway, and it is expected that the results will give more information on whether this viral disease in grouper can be classified as a newly listed disease for quarantine purposes. Based on the Minister of Agriculture Decree No. 520/Kpts/IK.220/B/1993, the significant diseases for quarantine purposes are shown in Table 1.

- Public health issues/zoonoses

Fish and fishery products are susceptible to physical, chemical and microbiological contamination. There was one reported outbreak of human poisoning following consumption of *Sardinella* sp. and *Selaroides leptolepis*, which was thought to be due to an unidentified toxic red-tide organism. Four deaths and 191 cases of illness were reported in November 1983 in East Flores, but detailed information was lacking. Problems with coliform contamination of molluscs have also been reported in some areas notably with green mussel (*Perna viridis*) around Jakarta Bay. No information is available on occurrence of residues in marine or freshwater fisheries products (Adisukresno, 1992). A research study reported that *Salmonella* spp. (*Salmonella arizona*, *S. paratiphy* A, B, C, D, E; and *S. lexington*) had been isolated from frog leg in Indonesia. Other bacterial contamination reported *Vibrio cholerae* found in frozen/shrimp to be exported in 1983, leading to rejection of 25 tonnes of frozen shrimp out of 46 tonnes sent from East Kalimantan (Heruwati, 1988).

Recently, in January 1995, some zoonotic diseases were reported at a Seminar on Quarantinable Fish Pests and Disease held in Indonesia. The diseases were mainly caused by parasites transmitted through freshwater fish, such as *Gnathostoma spinigerum, Capillaria philippinensis,* Heterophyidae and *Opisthorchis*. No cases were reported from marine fish, although marine fish could carry larvae of *Anisakis* I and *Terranova* type A, probably causing anisakiasis. Nevertheless, cases in humans in Indonesia would be very rare even it parasitic infections are high, because most people do not usually include raw fish in their diet (Kosin, 1995). A case of gnathostomiasis with source of infection in the freshwater fish *Channa striata* was also reported (Idris, 1995), as well as anisakiasis caused by nematode larvae of the family Anisakidae. The parasite frequently reported was larvae of *Anisakis* type I found in some marine fish (Ilahudae, 1995).

It has been agreed that in the near future a special meeting on zoonoses should be organized involving some related institutions. This would be a consideration as to whether zoonoses should be listed as additional quarantinable fish disease based on the Minister of Agriculture Decree No. 520/Kpts/IK.220/8/1993.

Recommendations for strengthening national programs in aquatic animal health certification and quarantine procedures

The objectives of the national policy for eradication of pests and diseases in Indonesia are:

- to protect fishery resources from damage;
- to prevent the spread of pests and diseases of fish;
- to avoid or to reduce economic losses ; and
- to support the effort of increasing aquaculture production.
- To fulfill the above objectives, development programs should include:

Training of fish quarantine inspectors and specialists, especially in diagnosis, prevention, treatment of fish diseases, fish biology, fish physiology, water quality management *etc*. through training courses, comparative field study and formal education.

Improvement and standardization of diagnostic techniques, prevention and treatment of fish diseases;

Improvement of diagnostic laboratory facilities, particularly for quicker and more accurate diagnoses of suspected diseases.

Further development of laws and regulations, including:

- Government Regulations;

- President Decree and its Implementation Guidelines;
- Minister of Agriculture Decree and Implementation Guidelines; and
- Instruction and Technical Guidelines.

Pest Risk Analysis (PRA) has been applied by to plant quarantine (Surahmat and Soeparno,1995) to guide quarantine recommendations, based on biological and economic analysis and consultation. Application of such analysis to aquatic animal quarantine should be explored.

Although the socio-economic importance of fish diseases has been well recognized, there is still only limited information available for rapid/accurate diagnosis, prevention and proper treatment of aquatic fish diseases, especially viral diseases in terms of :

- the pathogenicity of different viruses and viral strains;
- changes in viral virulence;

and it is therefore recommended that priority be given to further upgrading the existing facilities in all related institutions (quarantine, fishery service, university and research laboratory) for such work.

The Central Research Institute for Fisheries (CRIFI) with its mandate/role to establish and implement fisheries research and development also needs some basic supporting data from universities, the technical implementing units of the Directorate General of Fisheries, Indonesian Scientific Institute, SEAMEO-BIOTROP, and other scientific institutions. Cooperation among such bodies in aquatic animal health and quarantine should be promoted.

The development of international agreements and protocols for fish quarantine systems and procedures following OIE recommendations.

References

Adisukresno, S. (1992). Fish diseases and fish health management in Indonesia. Proceedings of the Symposium on Tropical Fish Health Management in Aquaculture. SEAMEO- BIOTROP, Bogor.

CAQ (1993). The Sixth Five Year Development Plan of Fish Quarantine. Centre for Agricultural Quarantine, Jakarta (in Bahasa Indonesia).

CAQ (1995). Result of the seminar on pests and diseases in fish quarantine. 24-26 January 1995, Centre for Agricultural Quarantine, Jakarta, Indonesia. Centre for Agricultural Quarantine, Jakarta.

Cholik, F. (1992). The support of research towards determination of fish quarantinable diseases. Paper presented at the Fish Quarantine Seminar, 20-22 October 1992, Bogor, Indonesia. (in Bahasa Indonesia)

CRIFI (1995). Introducing the Central Research Institute of Fisheries (CRIFI). Agency for Agricultural Research and Development (AARD), Ministry of Agriculture, Jakarta.

Davy, F.B. and Chouinard, A. (eds.) (1983). Fish Quarantine and Fish Diseases in Southeast Asia. Report of a workshop held in Jakarta, Indoneisa, 7-10 December 1982, International Development Research Centre, Ottawa, IDRC-210e, 79p.

Eny Budi Sri Haryani (1995). Fish health problems and fish quarantine system in Indonesia. Country report for the Group Training Course in Fish Physiology and Prevention of Epizootics. Sponsored by JICA and the Centre for Agricultural Quarantine, Indonesia.

Heruwati, E.S. (1988). The occurrence of contamination in fishery products. Workshop on Contamination of Food Monitoring. Department of Health of the Republic of Indonesia and FAO.

Idris, K.N. (1995). Snakehead (*Ophicephalus striatus*) as source of infection of gnathostomiasis. Paper prepared for the Seminar on Fish Quarantine, 4-27 January, 1995, Cipanas, Cianjur, Indonesia. Faculty of Medicine, University of Indonesia. (in Bahasa Indonesia).

Ilahude, H.D. (1995). Study on Anisakidae larvae of marine fish in Indonesia. Paper prepared for the Seminar on Fish Quarantine, 24-27 January, 1995, Cipanas, Cianjur, Indonesia. Parasitology Section, Faculty of Medicine, University of Indonesia. (in Bahasa Indonesia).

Kosin, E. (1995). Zoonoses transmitted via fish in Indonesia and the present treatment. Paper prepared for the Seminar on Fish Quarantine, 24-27 January, 1995, Cipanas, Cianjur, Indonesia. Parasitology Section, Faculty of Medicine, University of Indonesia. (in Bahasa Indonesia).

Ministry of Agriculture (1993). Minister of Agriculture Decree, No.520/KPTS/IK.220/8/1993 on List of Fish Quarantinable Pests and Diseases and their Carriers/media. Issued in Jakarta, 5 August 1993 (subject to addition/correction of listed diseases).

Owens, L. (1994). Sleepy grouper disease in Indonesia. A report prepared by the Department of Biomedical and Tropical Veterinary Sciences. James Cook University of North Queensland, Townsville, Australia.

Rukyani, A. (1993). The status of aquaculture and fish disease problems in Indonesia. Paper presented to the International Workshop and Training Course on Quick Diagnostic Methods and Bioecological Control of Fish and Shrimp Diseases. 29 July-7 August, 1993, Hanoi, Vietnam.

Surahmat and Soeparno (1995). What is Pest Risk Analysis (PRA)?. Paper presented at the Seminar on Fish Quarantine. 24-26 January 1995, Centre for Agricultural Quarantine, Jakarta, Indonesia. Centre for Agricultural Quarantine, Jakarta.

Taufik, A. (1995). Personal communication. Research Institute for Coastal Fisheries, Maros, South Sulawesi, Indonesia.

Table 1: Diseases considered significant for quarantine purposes (Ministry of Agriculture, 1993; as of January 1996)

Name of disease	Infectious agent	Class
Virus		
Channel catfish virus (CCV)	Ictaluri herpes virus	I
Spring viraemia of carp (SVC) and swimbladder inflammation (infectious carp dropsy)	Rhabdovirus carpio	I
Infectious pancreatic necrosis (IPN)	Birnavirus	I
Infectious haematopoeitic necrosis (IHN)	Rhabdovirus	I
Lymphocystis	Iridovirus	I
Infectious hypodermal and haematopoeitic necrosi (IHHN)*	Parvo-like virus	I
Hepatopancreas parvo-like virus (HPV)	Parvo-like virus	I
Baculovirus penaei (BP)*	Baculovirus	I
Monodon baculovirus (MBV)*	Monodon baculovirus	I
Baculovirus midgut-gland necrosis virus (BMNV)	BMN virus	I

Table 1. Continued.

Name of disease	Infectious agent	Class
Yellowhead virus (YHV) (to be listed)*	Baculovirus	I
Bacteria		
Furuncolosis*	*Aeromonas salmonicida*	I
Bacterial Kidney Disease (BKD)	*Renibacterium salmoninarum*	I
Tuberculosis (Mycobacteriosis)*	*Mycobacterium*	I
Nocardiasis	*Nocardia*	I
Edwardsiellosis*	*Edwardsiella tarda*	II
Emphisemateous putrative disease of catfish (EPDC)		I
Enteric septicaemia of catfish (ESC)	*Edwardsiella ictaluri*	II
Streptococciosis*	*Streptococcus* spp.	I
Pasteurellosis	*Pasteurella piscicida*	I
Enteric Red Mouth Disease (ERM)	*Yersinia ruckeri*	I
Gaffkemia	*Aerococcus viridansvar*	I
Parasites		
Whirling disease	*Myxobolus* (=*Myxosoma*) *cerebralis*	II
Pleistophorosis*	*Pleistophora hyphessobryconis*	I
Pleistophorosis	*Pleistophora anguillarum*	I
Ceratomyxosis	*Ceratomyxa shasta*	I
Henneguyan disease	*Henneguya exilis*	I
Cotton shrimp disease	*Thelohania duorara*	I
Cotton shrimp disease	*Thelohania penaei*	I
Bonamiosis	*Bonamia ostreae*	I
Haplosporidiosis	*Haplosporidium nelsonii*	I
Haplosporidiosis	*Haplosporidium costale*	I
Marteiliasis	*Marteilia refringens*	I
Perkensiasis	*Perkinsus marinus*	I
Ergasiliasis	*Ergasilus sieboldi*	II
White tumour disease*	*Nosema sp.*	I
Lytocestosis*	*Lytocestrus parvulus*	II
Paragonimiasis (to be listed)	*Paragonimus pulmonalis*	?

Table 1. Continued.

Name of disease	Infectious agent	Class
Fungus		
Sand paper disease	*Ichthyophonus hoferi*	I
Branchiomycosis	*Branchio sanguinis*	I
Aphanomycosis*	Aphanomyces	I

** = pathogen has been detected in Indonesia.*

Class I diseases cannot yet be eliminated from carriers/media.

Class II diseases may be eliminated/controlled by treatment

Japan

Kazuhiro Nakajima
National Research Institute of Aquaculture
Mie, Japan

Abstract

In Japan, there are no fish quarantine laws or regulations at present. However, the Fisheries Agency has advised prefecture governors to take various steps to avoid introduction of serious aquatic animal pathogens from abroad. There have been some disease outbreaks in aquaculture which may have arisen from introduction of aquatic animal pathogens. Regional activities to collect and disseminate information on the occurrence of aquatic animal diseases should be strengthened.

Introduction

In Japan, total fishery production in 1993 was 8,710,000 tonnes. The amount of production by aquaculture in 1993 was 1,360,000 tonnes, amounting to 15.6% of the total fisheries production.

Culture of marine finfishes amounted to 259,273 tonnes in 1993. Yellowtail (*Seriola quinqueradiata*) was the most important species in volume, with 141,646 tonnes, followed by the red seabream (*Pagrus major*) (Table 1). Apart from marine finfish, 478,590 tonnes of mollusc, such as oyster (Ostreidae) and common scallop (*Pactinopecten yessoensis*) and 1,712 tonnes of kuruma prawn (*Penaeus japonicus*) were produced in 1993.

International and in-country trade in aquatic organisms

Importation of fishery-product in 1993 was 3.1 million tonnes. Major imported fish are cod, pollack, salmon, trout, skipjack, shrimp, prawn, crab and so on. Fisheries product exports in 1993 were 0.4 million tonnes.

Current status of aquatic animal health certification and quarantine programmes

In Japan, there are no fish quarantine laws or regulations at present. However, in order to avoid the introduction of pathogens from abroad, the Fisheries Agency has requested prefecture governors to take appropriate steps. For example, when importing live eggs of salmonids for aquaculture, import dealers are requested to: a) ensure the shipment has a health certificate issued by the government of exporting countries; b) carry out an examination for pathogens at the time of importation; and c) disinfect the eggs immediately after importation. The Fisheries Agency entrusts the examination for pathogens at the time of importation to the Japan Fisheries Resource Conservation Agency.

Information on problems caused by introduction and transfers of aquatic organisms

Infectious pancreatic necrosis (IPN), infectious hematopoietic necrosis (IHN) and bacterial kidney disease (BKD) are diseases considered to have been introduced from abroad. Both IHN and BKD are thought to have entered through eggs imported for ranching, while IPN probably entered through eggs imported for culture. These diseases have become prevalent in salmonid farms and are causing severe damage to salmonid production.

In 1993, a new viral disease occurred at shrimp farms in Japan. High mortality of more than 80% in severe cases occurred among kuruma shrimps (*Penaeus japonicus*). Abnormal red coloration or discoloration and white spots on the body were characteristic signs of moribund shrimps. By normal histopathology, degenerated cells were observed in various tissues. The most characteristic feature of infection was degenerated nuclei in cuticular epidermal cells of the stomach or the lymphoid organ. The virus is tentatively designated RV-PJ, rod shaped nuclear virus of *Penaeus japonicus*. The virus is also thought to have entered with imported shrimps.

Recommendations for strengthening national programs in aquatic animal health certification and quarantine procedures

Regional activities to collect and disseminate information on the occurrence of aquatic animal diseases should be strengthened in cooperation with the Office International des Epitooties (OIE).

Table 1: Production of major marine aquaculture species in Japan in 1993

Species	Production (tonnes)
Finfish	
Yellowtail	141,646
Red seabream	72,696
Coho salmon	21,148
Horse mackerel	6,454
Shellfish	
Oyster	235,531
Common scallop	241,426
Shrimp	
Kuruma shrimp	1,712
Seaweed	
Laver	

Malaysia

A.K. Ismail and T.T. Chuah
Fisheries Research Institute
11960 Batu Maung, Penang
Malaysia

Abstract

Aquaculture in Malaysia has grown quickly in recent years. The government recognizes the potential economic impact from introduction of new aquatic animal pathogens and the Department of Fisheries is in the process of establishing a fish quarantine system. The effectiveness of national fish quarantine systems can be enhanced by regional standardization of guidelines and procedures that promote trade, human resource development and exchange of information.

Introduction

The fishery sector is important in Malaysia, as it supplies almost 60 % of the total animal protein intake of the population. The annual fish landings now average about one million tonnes. As the fishery products from the sea are not expected to increase any further, aquaculture will assume a greater role to increase fish supply and is expected in the future to contribute more than its present 10 % of fisheries production.

Aquaculture development in Malaysia has been rapid in recent years. The fastest expansion is in the cage culture sector, where there has been a doubling of area within the past four years in both freshwater and brackishwater environments (Table 1). Shrimp culture will pick up very soon, as there are a few big projects presently being implemented in Kerpan, Kedah and Tawau, Sabah. In 1993, a total of 103,723 tonnes of fish and shellfish was produced from aquaculture, which almost doubled the production in 1990. The bulk of the increase was from brackish water (90,400 tonnes) rather than from fresh water (13,323 tonnes). Perhaps influenced by consumer preference, freshwater aquaculture has performed relatively poorly over the years. In fact, there was reduced production in most of the species under culture, except for significant growth in black tilapia (1787 %), eel (537 %), freshwater catfish (266 %) and red tilapia (66 %), as seen in Table 2. In 1993, the total wholesale value of freshwater fish was RM 103.8 million[1], an increase of 78 % compared to 1990, with the export of eel being the main contributing factor. Overall, the freshwater fish supply increased by only 36 % during 1990-1993.

In brackishwater aquaculture, cockles contributed 86% to a combined

[1] RM 2.54 = 1 US$ in September 1997.

production of 90,400 tonnes in 1993 and registered a 116% increase compared to 1990 (Table 3). Among the finfish in marine cage culture, grouper had the fastest growth in production (633%). However, value-wise, the black tiger shrimp was most important, with an estimated wholesale value of RM 66.0 million, followed by cockles (RM 40.8 million), seabass (RM 38.0 million) and grouper (RM 26.4 million). In a time span of four years, brackishwater production doubled from 42,614 tonnes to 90,400 tonnes valued at RM 194.5 million in 1993.

International and in-country trade of aquatic organisms

Malaysia is still a net importer of fishery products in volume. In 1993, a total of 262,000 tonnes of fish and fishery products were imported while exports amounted to 206,000 tonnes. Value-wise, there was a surplus in international trade with the export value at US$ 314 million compared to an import value of US$ 271 million (at 1993 exchange rates).

From 1990 to 1993, the export volume and value of fishery products increased steadily following a rise in the exports of live food fish, aquarium fish, fresh/chilled tuna and processed shrimp. However, live fish accounted for only 10 % of the total export value of RM 800 million in 1993. The bulk of the fresh/frozen exports consisted of shrimp (26.3 % in value) captured from the sea. Pond cultured shrimp was mainly sold in the international market due to their high value. Singapore was the main export outlet in 1993 (71,058 tonnes or 34.5 %), but value-wise Japan ranked top due to high value of the exported processed shrimp and sashimi grade tuna. The other major markets for Malaysian fishery products are the U.S.A., Australia, Hong Kong and the Netherlands (Table 4).

As Malaysia has a high per caput consumption of seafood (45-50 kg), various fishery products are being imported every year to meet the high domestic demand. In 1993, the import value had increased to RM 690.8 million compared to RM 405.5 million in 1990 (Table 5). The main suppliers to Malaysia are Thailand, Indonesia, Japan and Taiwan.

Current status of aquatic animal quarantine and health certification programs

The expansion of the aquaculture industry has resulted in an increased cross-border trade of live fishes and other aquatic organisms. With such large and rapid movements, the danger of introduction of exogenous fish pathogens also increases. A survey conducted by Wong and Leong (1986) indicated that some of the imported marine fish fry harbored organisms pathogenic to fish.

In view of the potential threat posed by infectious fish diseases through the inadvertent importation of fish pathogens, the Department of Fisheries has planned to establish fish quarantine system in Malaysia (Shaharom, 1987).

However, it was only realized under the Sixth Malaysia Plan (1991-1995). To date, three Fish Health and Quarantine Centres are operational, starting with the one at Subang International Airport in Selangor (1991), followed by Glugor, Penang (1993) and Tampoi, Johor (1993). A fourth Centre will be built this year at Bukit Kayu Hitam, Kedah.

These centres are established to cater for the requirements of fish quarantine as well as facilitating live fish exports, mainly through the issuance of export permits and health certificates (Ismail and Siti Zahrah, 1993). Among the major functions of the Centres are:

- To carry out fish inspection and quarantine procedures on imported live fish consignments.
- To carry out regular inspections on the health status and sanitary conditions of fish farms, especially of those whose produce are for export.
- To carry out inspection of live fish consignments for export upon which health certificates are issued.
- To process applications for export and import permits.
- To ensure species listed under CITES are not traded.
- To render extension services in fish disease diagnosis and treatment.

The Department of Fisheries has been given the mandate to draw up rules and regulations to control the in-coming and out-going movements of live fish in the country. The department has initiated efforts to amend the Fisheries Acts 1985 to include quarantine regulations, so as to give the operation a legal status that is needed for effective implementation. Upon completion of the draft on the proposed quarantine regulations, a dialogue will be called for the relevant industry to review and comment, so that the quarantine system will be acceptable to all concerned groups. At present, all health certificates for live fish export are signed by the quarantine officer or designated personnel gazetted by the Department of Fisheries. During the initial stage, the Quarantine Centres confine their functions to mainly facilitate the exports of live fishery commodities. They ensure that all live fish consignments for export conform to the sanitary and health requirements of the importing countries. Upon request, health certificates are issued following the set procedures. The department plans to implement an accreditation scheme whereby fish farms found to be free from harmful fish pathogens will be certified.

Permits for both import and export of live fish are issued from the Quarantine Centres or the respective State Fisheries Offices. The procedures to apply for these permits are somewhat different. Generally, more stringent measures are taken to guard against the importation of undesirable diseased stocks and fish pathogens through either quarantine, detention, confiscation or destruction of the in-coming consignments in order to minimize this potential risk. A 14-day period of quarantine is considered sufficient for any disease problem to manifest itself. The bulk of the stock, which has been kept in a quarantine area at the importer's premises, can then be released after notification that the quarantine officer is satisfied with the health status of the stock concerned. It is a pre-requisite for each consignment of live fish to come with a health certificate issued by the designated authorities from the exporting countries.

Similarly, the exporters must maintain their culture premises in a hygienic condition and ensure that the fish stocks are healthy before a permit or health certificate is issued. After packing, the export consignment should come to the Quarantine Centre for final checking. If found to be satisfactory, the quarantine officer will then seal the boxes and issue the health certificate. If manpower allows, a staff could even be dispatched to help in custom s clearance at the airport.

For movement of live fish between East and West Malaysia, the consignor has to submit a similar application form and documents as required to obtain a letter of approval from the Centres or the respective State Fisheries Offices. Failure to do so will result in the consignment being refused entry by the Customs Authority at the receiving end. The same practice is applicable for movements between Sarawak, Sabah and the federal territory in Labuan. All Quarantine Centres are built with facilities to quarantine live fishes coming in from abroad and a diagnostic laboratory to check for fish diseases. At this early stage of implementation, constant up grading and improvement of the facilities are being made. Currently, fish disease diagnosis involving parasitology and bacteriology is conducted by the research division of the Department of Fisheries, which has five facilities, located at:

- Glugor, Penang.
- Batu Berendam, Malacca.
- Gelang Patah, Johor.
- Tanjung Demong, Terengganu.
- Pulau Sayak, Kedah.

However, most academic institutions in the country, notably the National Agriculture University (UPM) Serdang and University of Science (USM), have excellent diagnostic capabilities, both in terms of facilities and expertise in fish diseases. The Department of Veterinary Services, which has seven well-equipped diagnostic laboratories, including the Veterinary Research Institute in Ipoh, also provides fish disease diagnostic services to the fish farmers in the region.

Problems caused by the introduction and transfer of aquatic organisms

Under the Sixth Malaysia Plan, the Department of Fisheries, in an attempt to diversify coastal resources as to supply cheap animal protein to the local people, initiated a transplantation program of green mussels (*Perna viridis*) from their natural spatfall areas to other parts of the country. Since then, a few new raft culture areas of mussels have been established and they seem to be self-sustaining, with natural spatfall being observed later. So far, no negative effect has been reported.

However, Shaharom (1985) detected exotic *Sanguinicola* sp. in some of the Chinese carp fry imported to Malaysia. To date, incidences of mass mortalities in marine cage culture with imported seabass fry remain to be solved.

The outbreak of Epizootic Ulcerative Syndrome in the 1980s was a pertinent case that could perhaps be blamed on the unrestricted movements and trade of live fish in South East Asia (Lilley et al., 1992). In Malaysia, the first fish kills from EUS occurred in the Bekok river system in Johor State in 1979-80. Then in 1980-81, a severe ulcerative condition known as "wabak kudis" was evident among fish in the rice growing northern states of Perak, Penang and Kedah. Beside snakeskin gourami, *Trichogaster pectoralis,* which was the most commercially important paddy field fish affected, snakeheads, catfish, climbing perch, barbs and spiny eels also suffered high mortalities (Shariff and Low, 1980).

Recommendations for strengthening national programs in aquatic animal health certification and quarantine procedures

- Legislative requirements

At present there are no international regulations governing the movement of fish and fish products (de Kinkelin and Hedrick, 1991). The absence of regulations and ineffective implementation of fish quarantine systems, especially in the Asia-Pacific Region, is a serious matter of concern as the international trade of live fishes keeps increasing. A concerted effort to standardize guidelines and procedures in the implementation of quarantine systems will be beneficial to all parties concerned. As it requires a legal framework to enforce, the formulation of quarantine regulations should consider the views of those involved in fish production and trade in order to strike a balance between the requirements of both parties. While posing as a vanguard to protect the aquaculture industry from the attack of exogenous fish pathogens, the regulations imposed, however, should not backfire and hinder the development of the industry or threaten the livelihood of live fish traders.

- Infrastructure/human resources development

Shariff (1987) has identified several causes that contributed to the ineffectiveness of fish quarantine and certification systems in countries of this region. Among these are limited funds for the establishment and implementation of such a system, as well as a lack of qualified personnel to conduct fish disease inspection and diagnosis. Malaysia is facing such problems at the moment.

Under the Sixth Malaysia Plan (1991-1995), only four Quarantine Centers would be built at selected sites in Peninsular Malaysia. Although there are plans to establish more Centers or sub-stations at some other ports of entry, it will take time to see them come true. But this situation could be mitigated and put under control administratively through organizational set up and deployment of staff.

Active participation and strong support from relevant authorities/departments and research institutions directly involved with fish diseases and their diagnosis are essential to make the quarantine system work. The required support includes provision of a sufficient number of trained scientific and technical personnel, specialized and well-equipped laboratory facilities, and an adequate budget and administrative apparatus to implement the regulations.

- Requirements and interest in regional program to meet national needs

As the live fish trade is global in nature, a regional planning and coordinating body is deemed necessary for liaison purposes and to encourage constant exchange of information among the officers involved. Such collaboration among ASEAN countries will further enhance the effectiveness of fish quarantine systems in the region. Established linkages could be put to useful gains through e-mail or ordinary correspondence. A lead center with a core of expertise in various disciplines of fish diseases and well equipped diagnostic and training facilities could cater to the need for trained manpower and make fish quarantine systems a success in the region.

Acknowledgments

The authors wish to express thanks to the Director-General of Fisheries Malaysia for granting the permission to present this paper at this Workshop.

References

Annual Fisheries Statistics. (1990-93). Department of Fisheries Malaysia. Kuala Lumpur.

de Kinkelin, P. and Hedrick, R.P. (1991). International veterinary guidelines for the transport of live fish or live eggs. Annual Review of Fish Diseases, 1991: 27-40.

Ismail, A.K. and Siti Zahrah, A. (1993). Fish quarantine in Malaysia, p 61-69. In: Diseases in Aquaculture: the Current Issues. Eds R.P. Subasinghe and M. Shariff. Malaysian Fisheries Society, Kuala Lumpur.

Lilley, J.H., Phillips, M.J. and Tonguthai, K. (1992). A Review of Epizootic Ulcerative Syndrome (EUS) in Asia. Network of Aquaculture Centres in Asia-Pacific (NACA) and Aquatic Animal Health Research Institute (AAHRI), Bangkok. 73 p.

Shaharom, F. (1985). Parasitological examination of imported bighead carp (*Aristichthys nobilis*) and the grass carp (*Ctenopharyngodon idella*) in Peninsular Malaysia. Paper presented at a "Symposium on Practical Measures for Preventing and Controlling Fish Diseases", July 24-26, 1985, Bogor, Indonesia. 14 p. (Mimeo).

Shaharom, F.M. (1987). Fish quarantine and certification in Malaysia. In: Fish quarantine and fish diseases in South and Southeast Asia: 1986 Update. Ed. J.R. Arthur. Asian Fisheries Society Special Publication No. 1, 86p.

Shariff, M. and Low, A.T. (1980). An incidence of fish mortality in Bekok River, Johore, Malaysia. p. 153-162. *In* Proceedings of the International Symposium on Conservation Input from Life Sciences. 27-30 October 1980. Universiti Kebangsaan, Bangi, Selangor, Malaysia.

Shariff, M. (1987). Current status of programs for fish health certification and quarantine systems. In: Fish Quarantine and Fish Diseases in South and Southeast Asia: 1986 Update. Ed. J.R. Arthur. Asian Fisheries Society Special Publication No. 1, 86p.

Wong, S.Y. and Leong, T.S. (1986). Bacterial flora of seabass, *Lates calcarifer* Bloch, imported from Thailand for cage culture in Penang, Malaysia. p. 243-246. *In* The First Asian Fisheries Forum. Eds J.L. Maclean, L.B. Dixon and L.V. Hosillos. Asian Fisheries Society, Manila, Philippines.

Table 1: Aquaculture development in Malaysia (1990 - 1993)

		1993	1992	1991	1990
Inland	Ponds (ha)	4,347	5,598	4,861	4,285
	Ex-mining pool (ha)	1,397	1,059	644	641
	Cement tank (m^2)	34,794	29,046	24,613	21,413
	Cages (m^2)	48,693	29,046	24,613	21,4131
Coastal	Ponds (ha)	1,878	1,703	1,631	1,552
	Cages (m^2)	668,260	397,799	301,777	242,971

Source: Annual Fisheries Statistics. (1990-93). DoF, Malaysia.

Table 2: Freshwater aquaculture production and value by species (Q = tonnes; V = RM 1000 (estimated wholesale value))

Species		1993	1992	1991	1990
Eel	Q	2,824	1,572	443	*
(*Anguilla* sp.)	V	39,536	22, 008	6,195	*
Black tilapia	Q	3,774	3,146	2,690	200
(*Oreochromis mossambicus*)	V	25,264	20,814	17,997	13, 476
Red tilapia	Q	1,564	1,486	709	944
	V	7,874	5,885	3,059	3,481
Javanese carp	Q	1,400	2,505	2,064	1,790
(*Barbodes gonionotus*)	V	7,850	13,258	11,186	9,809

Table 2. Continued.

Species		1993	1992	1991	1990
Common carp	Q	972	1,703	1,499	1,282
(*Cyprinus carpio*)	V	6,739	15,118	13,404	9,426
River carp	Q	467	480	348	56
(*Leptobarbus hoevenii*)	V	5,680	3,710	2,566	4,154
Grass carp	Q	726	913	1,089	1,108
(*Ctenopharyngodon idella*)	V	3,085	4,085	4,686	4,855
Freshwater catfish	Q	722	904	912	197
(*Clarias* spp.)	V	2,655	4,676	1,704	54
Bighead carp	Q	169	1,221	730	763
(*Aristichthys nobilis*)	V	788	2,793	2,706	2,095
Goby	Q	36	39	14	419
Oxyeleotris marmoratus	V	767	769	300	3,531
Freshwater Prawn	Q	56	94	145	137
(*Macrobrachium rosenbergii*)	V	758	1,720	2,218	6,050
Total	Q	13,323	15,992	11,089	9,689
(including others)	V	103 831	103,248	71,707	58,281

*Indicates include under " others."

Table 3: Brackishwater aquaculture production and value by species. (Q = tonnes; V = RM 1000 (estimated wholesale value))

Species		1993	1992	1991	1990
Black tiger shrimp	Q	3,937	2,281	2,895	2,184
(*Penaeus monodon*)	V	66,060	46,260	50,032	40,982
Mud crab	Q	294	70	95	190
(*Scylla serrata*)	V	1,411	586	806	1,236
Banana shrimp	Q	57	141	162	155
(*P. m erguiensis*)	V	1,342	2,917	3,741	2,784
Seabass	Q	3,865	2,784	2,030	1,953
(*Lates calcarifer*)	V	37,967	25,571	18,562	16,969
Grouper	Q	1,056	288	154	144
(*Epinephelus* spp.)	V	26,441	7,648	2,987	1,991
Mangrove snapper	Q	841	281	98	414
(*Lutjanus argentimaculatus*)	V	9,461	2,857	921	2,462
Red snapper	Q	126	6	7	7
(*Lutjanus* spp.)	V	1,276	57	66	-
Others	Q	669	201	69	52
	V	8,178	1,725	447	na
Total fish	Q	10,796	6, 594	5,510	5,100
and crustaceans	V	152,289	87,621	77,622	59,000

Table 3. Continued.

Species		1993	1992	1991	1990
Cockle	Q	77,755	55,587	46,625	35,932
(*Anadara granosa*)	V	40,848	14,540	14,116	14,755
Green mussel	Q	1,812	1,493	1,563	1,582
(*Perna viridis*)	V	993	629	875	722
Oyster	Q	37	33	63	na
(*Crassostrea* spp.)	V	405	324	833	na
Total molluscs	Q	79,604	57,113	48,251	37,514
	V	42,246	15,493	15,824	15,477
Grand total	Q	90,400	63,707	53,761	42,614
	V	194,535	103,114	93,446	74,477

Table 4: Ten major export markets for Malaysian fishery products. (Quantity (Q) = tonnes; Value (V) = RM 1000)

Destination		1993	1992	1991	1990
Japan	Q	26,340	29,820	14,717	12,743
	V	264,897	210,854	181,542	134,015
Singapore	Q	71,085	61,450	57,580	60,823
	V	132,150	136,588	119,097	112,124
USA	Q	5,944	9,397	8 125	8,581
	V	61,629	71,975	97,155	93,185

Table 4. Continued.

Destination		1993	1992	1991	1990
Australia	Q	7,204	5,243	6,663	4,659
	V	59,014	57,605	75,855	68,581
Hong Kong	Q	3,883	6,702	4,152	4,331
	V	50,657	43,107	27,674	24,280
Netherlands	Q	2,680	3,817	3,351	2,770
	V	30,686	45,123	43,778	31,002
Italy	Q	2,177	1,775	1,379	388
	V	27,652	17,203	14,206	4,189
Spain	Q	2,042	2,940	2,064	1,990
	V	27,038	35,239	28,710	27,042
Thailand	Q	63,751	65,025	57,669	47,670
	V	22,797	32,151	28,048	21,044
UK	Q	2,351	2,299	2,460	1,566
	V	22,131	22,732	27,592	18,002
Grand total	Q	206,189	205,979	175,216	163,709
	V	800,734	765,510	739,651	630,002

*Indicates included under others."

Table 5: Imports of fishery products into Malaysia by country of origin. (Quantity (Q) = tonnes; Value (V) = RM 1000)

Origin		1993	1992	1991	1990
Thailand	Q	165,164	176,748	171,665	161,090
	V	306,245	295,555	202,992	171,494
Indonesia	Q	31,527	30,492	24,963	21,271
	V	127,281	104,868	85,824	73,543
Japan	Q	12,175	12,250	11,731	9,082
	V	48,247	45,323	39,983	28,056
Taiwan	Q	11,980	11,754	13,142	11,895
	V	48,088	47,401	25,224	19,009
India	Q	4,406	4,168	3,440	2,016
	V	23,024	22,484	21,024	14,064
New Zealand	Q	4,909	2,437	2,325	2,887
	V	19,586	17,283	16,745	12,449
Singapore	Q	4,303	4,427	3,795	3,390
	V	16,492	14,551	12,850	12,131
Chile	Q	6,331	2,863	3,413	4,944
	V	11,928	6,634	11,307	12,368
Australia	Q	1,586	614	418	369
	V	11,304	10,542	2,661	2,102
UK	Q	2,892	1,277	240	221
	V	10,939	4,997	2,950	2,917
Grand total	Q	261,630	259,881	226,256	228,549
	V	690,782	633,428	479,973	405,467

Nepal

Gopal ShresthaShrestha

Fisheries Development Division
Department of Agriculture, Central Fisheries Building
Balaju, Kathmandu
Nepal

Abstract

Nepal is a land-locked country that shares water and fisheries resources with surrounding countries. The fish disease Epizootic Ulcerative Syndrome (EUS) occurred in Nepal in 1989, causing economic damage to aquaculture. There is currently no aquatic animal quarantine law to control the import of pathogens in live fish and other aquatic animals into Nepal and existing capacity for disease diagnosis and control is limited. This paper gives recommendations for minimizing risks associated with movement of aquatic animals and for strengthening of capacity for aquatic animal health management.

Introduction

Nepal is a land-locked country, surrounded in the south, west and east by India, and in the north by the People's Republic of China. Geographically, the country can be divided into three regions: southern flat land called the Terai, the mid-hilly/mountain region, including some valleys, and the northern parts containing the high Himalayan ranges. Some of the perennial rivers of Nepal originate from Tibet, and similarly almost all of the rivers of Nepal become tributaries of the River Ganges of India. There are common fish species in these rivers and migration of fish between India and Nepal and *vice versa,* providing opportunities for interchange of pathogens and spread of fish diseases from one country to the other. Nepal also has an open border with India, so import of fish pathogens with fish seed and ornamental/aquarium fish is also possible. Ornamental/aquarium fish are imported by air from different parts of Asia, including Singapore, Hong Kong and Thailand, providing another possible source of pathogens, due to the lack of aquatic animal quarantine regulations.

Aquaculture activities are concentrated in the eastern and mid-central regions of the Terai at a semi-intensive level, whereas more intensive methods have been used in the western and far-western regions. At present, a program has been launched to stock advance-sized fingerlings in wetlands, promote cage/pen and pond culture and develop fisheries in lakes and reservoirs. Fish production has increased significantly in recent years. It is estimated that in 1995, fish production from capture fisheries of rivers, reservoirs and natural impoundments was about 10,000 tonnes. Aquaculture contributes about 11,000 tonnes of fish production, giving a total fish production for Nepal of around 21,000 tonnes in 1995.

Fisheries are impacted by several activities in Nepal. Besides unplanned urbanization, industrialization and pollution, there is a major problem of electrofishing, dynamiting and poisoning which destroys aquatic animal life and disrupts ecosystems in natural water bodies. Capture fisheries are declining due to over-fishing and illegal fishing. The Aquatic Animal Life Conservation Act was formulated in 1961 in order to control illegal fishing activities, such as electrofishing, dynamiting and poisoning in natural water bodies. This act has not been effective due to the lack of a proper identification of the enforcement/supervision authorization. Thus, the Fisheries Development Division has drafted a revision on the Aquatic Animal Life Conservation and Utilization Act, which has been forwarded to the Ministry of Agriculture for final approval by parliament.

International and in-country trade in aquatic organisms

About 50 million fish seed are transported within the country, the main sources being private and public hatcheries, nurseries and fish seed dealers. A few private fish dealers import fish seed from India. There is some export, including *Tor putitora* (mahseer), *Catla catla* (catla), *Ctenopharyngodon idella* (grass carp) and *Cyprinus carpio* (common carp). Prophylactic treatment for fish disease has been undertaken prior to export, however, overall quantities of exported fish seed are negligible, and there is no regular consignment. In addition to hatchery supplies, fish seed of the major carps *Labeo rohita* (rohu), *Cirrhina mrigala* (mrigal or naini) and catla are collected from the big rivers of India during the monsoon. This wild fish seed may be infected by one or more pathogens, leading to possible transmission of disease. In the Terai, some fish diseases found in aquaculture ponds appear similar to those affecting fish in northern India. During fish seed transportation, fish farms should use prophylactic measures.

One of the most serious fish diseases affecting Nepal is Epizootic Ulcerative Syndrome (EUS), which is believed to have been transmitted from abroad. The EUS outbreak in Nepal was recorded in early 1989 in the Morang and Sunsari districts of the Eastern Development Region of Nepal. Within one year, EUS spread throughout Jhapa, Morang, Sunsari, Saptari and Siraha districts of the same region, affecting roughly 328 ha of water area, primarily fish culture ponds. The disease then spread into the central and western region districts of Dhanusa, Mahottari, Sarlahi, Bara, Parsa, Rautahat, Makawanpur, Chitwan, Nawalparasi, Rupendehi, Kapilbastu, Kailali and Kanchanpur by the following year. By 1993, EUS had spread to the sub-temperate lakes, ponds and rice fields of the mid hills, where wild indigenous fish species were affected.

Now this disease has spread throughout all aquaculture areas except cold water fisheries.

Current status of aquatic animal quarantine and health certification programs

During the EUS outbreak in 1989, His Majesty's Government of Nepal ordered checks on the health of imported fishes through the Plant Quarantine Offices, already established at important entry points. These offices are for plants and crops and are not equipped to cover fish and fish products. At present, a Central Fish Disease Diagnosis Laboratory has been set up at the Central Fisheries Building in Balaju, Kathmandu to provide fish disease diagnosis.

There is currently no aquatic animal quarantine law to control the import of pathogens in live fish and other aquatic animals into Nepal. From the Central Fish Disease Diagnosis Laboratory, a regular check-up program could be launched at the main port of entry, Tribhuvan International Airport, Kathmandu.

Problems caused by the introduction and transfer of aquatic organisms

In the early 1960's monoculture was practiced with exotic species like common carp. During this time, the ectoparasites *Trichodina*, *Argulus* and *Ichthyophthirius* and monogenetic helminths were reported in various public fish farms. In the very beginning, fish culture was practiced as a hobby by big farmers, with indigenous major carp, rohu, mrigal (or naini), and catla (or bhakur). During the mid 1960s and 1970s, four other carp species, grass carp, silver carp (*Hypophthalmichthys molitrix*) and bighead carp (*Aristichthys nobilis*) were introduced for polyculture. A digenetic trematode was reported from these carps in 1968 and 1970. Nile tilapia (*Oreochromis niloticus*) and *Puntius* spp. have also been introduced for research purposes, but as of now these fish have not been released into the private sector.

In 1988, about 50,000 fertilized eggs of rainbow trout (*Oncorhynchus mykiss*) were introduced from Japan for coldwater fisheries and raceway culture. A disease, believed to be Infectious Pancreatic Necrosis (IPN), has appeared in some of these fish. So, in this manner, we have imported an exotic fish as well as a pathogen. An aquatic animal quarantine act and regulation should be in place to counter such risks.

About 100 species of ornamental fish are imported by air from Southeast Asia, but no records of the number and species are available.

Frozen seafood imported by land and air may contain aquatic pathogenic organisms as well. However, there is little information on this subject.

Recommendations for strengthening national programs in aquatic animal health certification and quarantine procedures

As for plants and crops, a health certificate from the Fisheries Development Division or other authorized agencies should be required for the import and export of aquatic animals.

- Adequate manpower is required to run this program.
- A modest, properly equipped laboratory should be established in each of the five Development Regions. The laboratories should be utilized by health management services working at the grass roots level.
- Any aquatic organism, including fish seed, transported within the country should have a certificate indicating the organism as free of significant pathogens. The concerned central or regional authority should issue this certificate.
- The affected country should immediately report the appearance of any new pathogen to NACA/AAHRI so that all member countries can be advised.

Philippines

Melba Reantaso

Senior Aquaculturist
Bureau of Fisheries and Aquatic Resources (BFAR)
Quezon City, Metro Manila,
Philippines

Abstract

The Philippines has extensive marine resources and good freshwater resources. Aquaculture is well developed and makes an important contribution to the economy of the country. There have been several ecological and economic problems caused by the introduction of exotic aquatic animals and a number of legal instruments exist to reduce the risks associated with introductions and transfers of aquatic animals. This paper makes recommendations to enhance aquatic animal health certification and quarantine programs consistent with the government commitment to the promotion of a more open international trading environment.

Introduction

The Philippines, being an island country, is endowed with great marine and inland resources. Marine resources cover a total territorial water area (including EEZ) of about 220,000,000 ha, consisting of 26,600,000 ha (or 12%) coastal and 193,400,000 ha (or 88%) oceanic areas; a shelf area of 18,460,000 ha (or 8%) with a depth of 200 m; coral reef area of 2,700,000 ha; and a coastline 17,460 km long. Inland resources consist of 338,393 ha of fresh and brackishwater swamplands; 253,845 ha of fresh and brackishwater fishponds; and 250,000 ha of other inland resources such as lakes (200,000 ha), rivers (31,000 ha) and reservoirs (19,000 ha) (Philippine Fisheries Profile, 1994).

Fisheries play an important role in improving the country's economy. In 1991, the Philippines was the second biggest producer of tuna and tuna-like fishes in the region next to Indonesia. In 1993, the country ranked 12th among the largest fish producers in the world (INFOFISH Fact Sheet, 1995). Philippine fisheries had a steady annual average growth rate of 3% from 1985 to 1994, equivalent to 11.2% growth rate in terms of value. The fishing industry provides livelihood to about 1 million Filipinos or 5% of the country's labor force.

In 1994, total fisheries production was 2.686 million tonnes valued at 81.299 billion pesos (1 US$ = 26.00 Ps, current exchange rate), an increase of 1.47% in quantity and 14.3% in value over the previous year. Municipal fisheries (fishing in coastal and inland waters with or without the use of boats of three gross tonnage or less) had a production share of 38% and a value share of 31%; commercial fisheries (fishing in the offshore waters with the use of fishing vessels more than 3 gross tonnes) had a share of 33% with a value share of 26%; while the aquaculture sector had the biggest value share of 43%, equivalent to 29% of the total fish production.

Major species produced from aquaculture are seaweeds, milkfish, tilapia and shrimp. Aquaculture production of milkfish and shrimp from brackishwater fishponds were 135,682 tonnes and 92,269 tonnes, respectively. Other species such as tilapia, white shrimp, grouper, sea bass, spadefish, siganids and mudcrab had a combined total production of 16,406 tonnes. Tilapia and carp cultured in freshwater ponds gave a total production of 38,923 tonnes, while other species such as catfish, mudfish and gourami produced a total of 7,959 tonnes. Production from fishpens in fresh and marine waters utilizing milkfish and tilapia gave a total of 40,279 tonnes, and 33,015 tonnes from fish cages in fresh and marine waters. Seaweed mariculture produced 403,856 tonnes; while oyster and mussel mariculture had a production of about 11,000 tonnes each. These figures indicate the importance of aquaculture to the country.

International and in-country trade in aquatic organisms

In 1994, total Philippine exports amounted to US$ 577.6 million, an increase of 6.8% from 1993. Major fishery exports include processed (frozen/chilled or in preparation) shrimps/prawn, tuna, seaweeds, cuttlefish/squid, crabs/crab fats, lobster, live ornamental fish, processed capiz shells and live grouper. Japan had the biggest share of the market (about 49.5%) followed by the USA (16.3%), Germany, Hong Kong, United Kingdom, Korea, South Africa, Canada, Netherlands and Taiwan. The share of Philippine exports of live fish (consisting of ornamental fish, eels, groupers, and other live fish) and other aquatic organisms (such as scallops, clams, arkshell, sea urchins and others) for 1995 was valued at US$ 105.9 million, a tremendous increase from US$ 6.5 million in 1991.

Importation of fish and fishery products in 1994, valued at US$ 94,521, increased by 11.4% over the previous year. Major fishery imports consist of chilled/frozen fish (such as tuna, sardines and mackerel) and flour meals and pellets of fish, crustaceans and mollusks unfit for human consumption. Importation of live fish (such as trout, carps, tilapias and other live fish) and other aquatic organisms (such as scallops and mussels) for 1994 amounted to US$ 23,491. There was a steady increase in the import of these commodities from 1991 (valued at US$ 3,623) to 1995 (valued at US$ 92,969).

Current status of aquatic animal quarantine and health certification programs

The Philippine government department and bureau mandated to recommend legislation/action on aquatic animal health quarantine and health certification programs is the Bureau of Fisheries and Aquatic Resources (BFAR), presently under the Department of Agriculture (DA). The legal mandates are embodied in Presidential Decree No. 704 dated May 16, 1975, and Section 13(c) of Executive Order No. 116 effective January 30, 1987. Under this mandate, the BFAR created several Fisheries Administrative Orders (or FAOs) concerning the exportation and importation of fish and fishery/products. An FAO is an official document pertaining to rules and regulations regarding all fishery and aquatic resources in the country duly endorsed by the BFAR Director and approved by the DA Secretary.

Existing legislation/actions on aquatic animal quarantine matters are contained in several FAOs, Executive Orders and Central Circulars. Important and relevant FAOs concerning exportation include the following:

1. FAO No. 117, series of 1975 "Rules and regulations governing the operation of processing plants for fish and fishery/aquatic products and prescribing/requiring standards, quality control and inspection of processed fish and fishery/aquatic products".
2. Section 36 of PD No. 704, series of 1975 "Banning the exportation of bangus fry".
3. FAO No. 147, series of 1984 "Rules and regulations governing the issuance of permits/commodity clearance for the exportation of fish and fishery/aquatic products".
4. Executive Order (EO) No. 1016, series of 1985 "Withdrawing the inspection, commodity and export clearance requirements on Philippine exports".
5. FAO No. 162, series of 1986 "Rules and regulations governing the issuance of permits for the exportation of live mud crabs (*Scylla serrata*)".
6. FAO No. 168, series of 1990 "Rules and regulations governing the gathering, culture and exportation of shelled mollusks (Phylum Mollusca)".
7. FAO No. 173, series of 1991 "Banning the exportation of bangus fingerlings".
8. FAO No. 143-5, series of 1993 "Amending Section 1, FAO No. 143-4 allowing the exportation of live pond-raised prawns not more than sixty (60) grams per piece".
9. FAO No. 185, series of 1993 "Ban on the taking, catching, selling, purchasing and possession, transporting and exporting of dolphins".

Important and relevant FAOs concerning importation include the following:

1. FAO No. 126, series of 1979 "Rules and regulations prohibiting the importation and/or possession of live piranha".
2. FAO No. 135, series of 1982 "Rules and regulations governing the importation of fish and fishery/aquatic products".
3. Executive Order No. 1073, effective January 1, 1986 "Prescribing safeguards for domestic industries upon the lifting of imports licensing for certain products".
4. FAO No. 183, series of 1992 "Prohibiting the importation of yellow fin tuna and tuna products from certain countries"
5. Central Bank Circular No. 1100, series of 1986 "Importation of commodity groups listed in Annex "A" hereof without prior approval of the Board of Investments and other government agencies".
6. Central Bank Circular No. 1356, dated September 25, 1992 "Implementation of items for which tariff adjustments had been made as approved under Executive Order No. 8, the importation of commodities listed in Annexes A and B hereof, no longer requires the prior approval of the government agencies concerned".
7. FAO No. 189, series of 1993 "Prohibiting the importation of live shrimp and prawn of all stages".

The main rules and regulations pertaining to quarantine, certification and other related policies are found in FAOs 147 (exportation) and 135 (importation). Natividad (1987) reviewed the procedures and implementation of quarantine and certification regulations embodied in the two FAOs. He reported that these regulations were weak and relatively devoid of technical reference. There are no specific and clear-cut regulations/procedures for fish disease control through quarantine and certification. In actual operation, the inspection procedure has provisions only for species identification and the general health condition based on visual examination of shipments. Particular emphasis is provided for banned/restricted, endangered and exotic species, based on other existing FAOs (see above listing).

The implementation of Central Bank Circular No. 1356, dated 25 September, 1992, removed the import requirements of concerned government agencies and only follows the required tariff adjustments approved under Executive Order No. 8. This development was aimed at removing import restrictions that affect international trade as part of the government's efforts to liberalize trade in order to promote economic recovery.

Decision making procedures with respect to approval of introductions and transfers of aquatic organisms are vested upon the BFAR. The Fisheries Regulatory and Quarantine Division of BFAR takes action on requests for approval of introductions and transfers of aquatic organisms upon consultation with concerned technical divisions/sections of the Bureau (e.g. Fishery Resources Research Division, Aquaculture Division, Fish Health Section).

In 1992, the Department of Agriculture created a national "Committee on the Introduction of Exotic Aquatic Organisms" by virtue of Special Order No. 642. The committee is composed of members from BFAR, the Philippine Council for Aquatic and Marine Research and Development (PCAMRD), the Southeast Asian Fisheries Development Center (SEAFDEC), and the University of the Philippines Marine Science Institute (UPMSI). The committee serves as an advisory body to the DA Secretary on matters concerning aquatic introductions.

The Fish Health Section of BFAR issues health certificates concerning the presence or absence of parasites for outgoing shipments of ornamental fish upon requirement of importing country. There are no existing quarantine facilities and expertise for aquatic animal health certification in any port of entry in the Philippines.

Problems caused by the introduction and transfer of aquatic organisms

In the Philippines, the introduction and transfer of aquatic species, mostly fish, were made for a variety of reasons. These include provision of more food fish for the country through introduction and transfer of fish in lakes and rivers, for aquaculture, for biological control of undesirable species such as mosquitoes and weeds, for sport fishing (Juliano et al., 1989) and for the ornamental fish trade.

The impacts of fish introduction, which may involve hybridization with endemic fish species, habitat and water quality deterioration, competition for space and food, predation, introduction of exotic parasites and diseases (Arthington, 1989) and displacement of native fish populations, have not been carefully and seriously considered at the time of introduction. This has resulted in some irreversible ecological, socio-economic and disease impacts. Each individual impact will be discussed in relation to introductions and transfers of fish and other aquatic organisms in the Philippines (see Table 1).

The introduction of two species of tilapia, Nile tilapia and Mossambique tilapia, to the country resulted to hybridization between the two species. Electrophoretic studies conducted by Macaranas et al. (1986) showed gene introgression in stocks of *Oreochromis niloticus* in the Philippines. The existence of genetically pure stocks of *O. niloticus* in the country is doubtful.

The transfer of a freshwater, carnivorous goby, *Glossogobius giurus*, to Lake Lanao, island of Mindanao was thought to be responsible for the depletion of the indigenous cyprinid population of the lake. The sailfin molly, *Poecilia latipinna*, originally intended for control of malarial mosquitoes, has now become a pest in brackishwater fishponds. The introduction of the exotic walking catfish, *Clarias batrachus*, resulted in successful establishment in Philippine lakes and rivers. However, the native freshwater catfish, *Clarias macrocephalus*, which possesses better food fish qualities, has been completely dominated by the walking catfish (Juliano et al., 1989).

The introduction of Mossambique tilapia, *Oreochromis mossambicus*, resulted in competition for food with *Chanos chanos* in brackishwater aquaculture (Juliano et al., 1989). Another negative impact of indiscriminate introduction of tilapia was the reduction in the population of native fishes, *Mistichthys luzonensis* (see Gindelberger, 1981; Soliman, 1993; and Mercene, 1995) and *Sardinella tawilis* (Mercene, 1995).

A classic example of the irreversible ecological and disease impact of careless introduction is the case of the golden snail, *Pomacea canaliculata*. This species not only displaced the Philippine native snail *Pila conica* but also became a major pest in ricefields (Acosta and Pullin, 1993).

With regards to introduction of exotic parasites, Table 2 shows that to date, a total of 14 species of exotic parasites have become established in the Philippines. These include five species of protozoans of the genera *Trichodina* (Duncan, 1977; Natividad et al., 1986; Bondad-Reantaso, 1989), *Tripartiella* (Bondad-Reantaso and Arthur, 1989), and *Trichodinella* (Duncan, 1977; Albaladejo and Arthur, 1989); six species of monogeneans belonging to the genera *Cichlidogyrus* (Duncan, 1973; Natividad et al., 1986; Bondad-Reantaso and Arthur, 1990), *Gyrodactylus* (Cone et al., 1995) and the endoparasitic *Enterogyrus* (Bondad-Reantaso and Arthur, 1990); one species of cestode, *Bothriocephalus* (Lopez, 1986; Lumanlan et al., 1990); one species of crustacean, *Lernaea* (Velasquez, 1984; Regidor and Arthur, 1986) and the parasitic glochidia of a freshwater bivalve, *Cristaria plicata* (Juliano et al., 1989; Bondad-Reantaso and Arthur, 1990). Although the effects of these introductions are unknown, and there are only very few reports of fish diseases caused by these parasites, most of these species have known pathogenicities.

In a survey of parasites of fishes imported into the Philippines, Albaladejo and Arthur (1989) and Lumanlan et al. (1990) provided evidence that fish entering the Philippines carried with them a myriad of potentially pathogenic parasites.

Epizootic ulcerative syndrome (EUS), still the most serious disease that has occurred in the Philippines affecting fresh (Llobrera, 1987) and brackishwater fish species (Reantaso, 1991), causing heavy mortalities in many wild stocks, was believed to have been introduced and spread through movement of live fish.

Although no scientific evidence is available, it was claimed that some diseases affecting local penaeid species may have been brought by penaeid shrimps, *Penaeus stylirostris* and *P. vannamei*, introduced to the Visayas in the Philippines from Latin America (Juliano et al., 1989).

Table 3 shows some information on the status of aquatic organisms introduced to the Pacific Islands from the Philippines (Eldredge, 1994). Some have shown successful establishment such as the Mossambique tilapia, the green mussel (*Perna viridis*) and some species of seaweeds; others have unknown status. There is so far no record of disease introduction, but this is probably more a reflection of insufficient surveillance rather than the lack of it.

Table 4 shows a partial list of zoonotic parasites occurring on fresh and marine fish species in the Philippines based on available literature. Many species of parasites causing nematode, cestode and trematode diseases have been reported but it is not clear whether these parasites were exotic or part of the native parasite fauna of Philippine fishes.

Recommendations for strengthening national programs in aquatic animal health certification and quarantine procedures

The following recommendations are presented to strengthen national programs towards aquatic animal health quarantine and certification:

- National program on aquatic animal health quarantine and certification

It is recommended that a working group/committee on aquatic animal health quarantine and certification program at the national level be formed. Its composition should include representatives from the government (DA, BFAR, PCAMRD, Fisheries Quarantine Officers, Department of Trade and Industry, Bureau of Customs), research institutes/academe (e.g. SEAFDEC, ICLARM, UP) and private sector (importers/exporters). The committee shall be responsible for raising the profile regarding aquatic animal health quarantine and certification and presenting a strong case for the preparation of legislation on this subject.

The case should include an account of the fish disease situation of the country, including the native disease fauna; listing and detailed knowledge of potential pathogens; economic impact of international trade of live fish and losses due to fish disease; evaluation of existing quarantine legislation, operation, facilities/expertise, and diagnostic and inspection/examination methods; trade restrictions and implications; and current developments (e.g. international "codes of practice", World Trade Organization agreements).

- Legislation requirements

A strong legal framework that will embody the rules and regulations under which a fisheries quarantine and certification program should operate is necessary. The mandate should stress the prevention of the introduction, establishment and spread of serious fish diseases within and outside the country. Technically sound implementation guidelines, adequate enforcement and corresponding laboratory services should support such legislation. The government has the responsibility to ensure that the private sector/public will have a clear understanding that such legislation is not just another bureaucratic procedure or trade barrier, but rather a strategy that is advantageous and that will benefit their industry.

- Infrastructure and human resources development

The Philippine government recognizes the importance of fish health management. The BFAR Fish Health Laboratory located in Manila, and now 10 years old, had survived the many internal problems common to government institutions of a developing country such as the Philippines. With financial support (for research, equipment, graduate studies and technical training) generously provided by world organizations such as the International Development Research Centre (IDRC) of Canada, the Network of Aquaculture Centres for Asia-Pacific (NACA), the Australian Centre for International Agricultural Research (ACIAR) and the Japanese Ministry of Education, to mention a few, a modest laboratory has been established, equipped with basic facilities needed for the operation of a fish health laboratory, and complemented with technically qualified manpower. However, the government needs to provide a permanent facility and more government support for research, extension and training to sustain the operation of a fish health laboratory that will largely support the national program on aquatic animal health quarantine and certification. Being an island country, it is also recommended that government fish health laboratories be established in strategic locations within the country. In addition, promotion of the establishment of fish health laboratories within the private sector is also desirable.

Continuous upgrading of research, diagnostic and extension capabilities of existing fish health staff is also required to enable them to undertake better diagnostic service to the industry, particularly the fish farmers; more accurate assessment of the fish disease situation and its economic impact; and improved training and extension service to fisheries extension officers, including farmers. These will enable the staff to be competent fish health professionals, and thereby sustain the financial and technical investments provided by the government and donor agencies.

There is an urgent need to provide appropriate technical training to quarantine and inspection officers stationed in all ports of entry in the Philippines, so that their operation will not be limited only to movement of restricted/banned, endangered and exotic species and administrative supervision of requirements for such movements, but extended to a working knowledge on fish diseases and the role of quarantine and certification program as a strategy to minimize the risk of introduction, establishment and spread of fish diseases.

There is also a need to professionalize the subject of fish health management. To start with, a strong curriculum on this subject should be incorporated into the curriculum of local universities offering degrees on fisheries, veterinary and biological studies. A possible graduate program on fish health may also be considered.

- Requirements/interest in a regional program to meet national needs

It is recommended that regional and world organizations continue to provide collaborative programs and strategies to countries of the region concerning aquatic animal health quarantine and certification. Collaborative programs may cover areas that will strengthen research and diagnostic capabilities, and assist in obtaining accurate information on aquatic animal disease situations, as well as economic assessments of aquatic animal health and disease control. Of paramount importance is that such collaboration should result in providing a better service to fish farmers, where they can maximize fish production through prevention of losses caused by fish disease.

Collaborative regional strategies should include evaluation of existing quarantine procedures, development of quarantine systems and standardization of diagnostic methods/procedures based on sharply defined areas of common regional interest. It is desirable that these strategies be based on existing international "codes of practice" defined by a regional body as applicable to the region. Regular monitoring of the implementation of such standardized procedures and other efforts is also required. The creation of a regional body or a working group using regional and international experts (with long experience in the region) is very important to serve as a strong technical support to existing and future regional programs on aquatic animal health quarantine and certification.

It was 18 years ago (see Davy and Graham, 1979) when the subject fish diseases in South East Asia was first discussed in a regional meeting held in Indonesia in 1978. Since then, there have followed a number of regional meetings to discuss issues concerning quarantine/certification and disease and other impacts of the international movement of aquatic organisms. It is hoped that this meeting will, apart from recognizing the need to address the above issues (as already recognized by all the other regional meetings), serve as a venue to make concrete plans and follow through its implementation. It is therefore a great challenge to world organizations and particularly regional organizations such as NACA, AAHRI-SEAADCP, SEAMEO-BIOTROP, SEAFDEC, AFS/FHS, universities and national governments, to put their acts together and harmoniously work towards achieving implementable strategies on aquatic animal health quarantine and certification.

Acknowledgments

I wish to thank BFAR Director Dennis B. Araullo and Asst. Dir. Atty. Reuben A. Ganaden for their kind support to my attendance at this workshop. I am also indebted to BFAR/DA quarantine officers for their participation in an informal discussion regarding the status of quarantine operation in the Philippines and my colleagues at the BFAR, Atty. R. de Sagun, Dr. J.D. Albaladejo, Ms. D. Ladra, Mr. E. Alesna, Ms. V. Luyun, Ms. M. Consulta and Ms. S. Regidor for providing useful information and reference materials. Support for attendance to this meeting provided by NACA and the South East Asian Aquatic Disease Control Project (SEAADCP) of the Aquatic Animal Health Research Institute (AAHRI), both based in Bangkok, Thailand, is greatly appreciated.

References

Acosta, B. O. and Pullin, R.S.V. (eds.) (1993). Environmental impact of the golden apple snail (*Pomacea* sp.) on the rice farming systems in the Philippines. Central Luzon State University and International Center for Living Aquatic Resources Management Publication. 34 p.

Africa, C.M. (1937). Evidence of intramuscular invasion in the life cycle of *Haplorchis yokogawai* (Katsuda, 1932), Chen, 1936 (Heterophyidae). J. Philipp. Isl. Med. Assoc. 17: 737-743.

Africa, C.M. (1938). An attempt to elucidate the filtration of eggs of certain heterophyid trematodes into the general circulation. Philipp. J. Animal Industry, 5: 187-201.

Albaladejo, J.D. and Arthur, J.R. (1989). Some trichodinids (Protozoa: Ciliophora: Peritrichida) from freshwater fishes imported into the Philippines. Asian Fish. Sci. 3: 1-25.

Arthington, A.H. (1989). Impacts of introduced and translocated freshwater fishes in Australia. p. 7-20. *In* Exotic Aquatic Organisms in Asia. S.S. De Silva. (ed.) Asian Fisheries Society Special Publication 3, Asian Fisheries Society, Manila, Philippines.

Bondad-Reantaso, M.G. and Arthur, J.R. (1989). Trichodinids (Protozoa: Ciliophora: Peritrichida) of Nile tilapia (*Oreochromis niloticus*) in the Philippines. Asian Fish. Sci. 3: 27-44.

Bondad-Reantaso, M.G. and Arthur, J.R. (1990). The parasites of Nile tilapia (*Oreochromis niloticus* (L.)) in the Philippines, including an analysis of changes in the parasite fauna of cultured tilapia from fry to marketable size. p. 729-734. *In* The Second Asian Fisheries Forum. R. Hirano and I. Hanyu. (eds.) Asian Fisheries Society, Manila, Philippines.

Cabrera, B.D. (1968). Anisakiasis - will it become a public health problem in the Philippines? Editorial. Acta Med. Philippina, 4, Ser. 2, No. 4: 214-215.

Cabrera, B.D. Baltazar, R., Caviles, A.P. Domingo, E., Gonzaga, A., Lingao, A. and Campos, P.C. (1969). *Capillaria philippinensis* eggs demonstrated in fish from Pudoc, Ilocos Sur. J. Philipp. Med. Assoc. 45:275-280.

Cone, D.K., Arthur, J.A. and Bondad-Reantaso, M.G. (1995). Description of two new species of *Gyrodactylus* von Nordmann, 1832 (Monogenea) from cultured Nile tilapia, *Tilapia nilotica* (Cichlidae), in the Philippines. J. Helmin. Soc. Wash. 62: 6-9.

Cross, J.H., Banzon, T., Clarke, M.D., Basaca-Servilla, V., Watten, R.H. and Dizon, J.J. (1972). Studies on the experimental transmission of *Capillaria philippinensis* in monkeys. Trans. Roy. Soc. Trop. Med. Hyg. 66: 819-827.

Cross, J.H., Banzon, T. and Singson, C. (1978). Further studies on *Capillaria philippinensis*: development of the parasite in the Mongolian gerbil. J. Parasitol. 64: 208-213.

Davy, B. and Graham, M. (eds.) (1979). Diseases of fish cultured for food in South East Asia. Report of a workshop held in Jakarta, Indonesia, 28 November - 1 December 1978. International Development Research Center Publication IDRC-139e. 32 p.

Duncan, B.L. (1973). *Cichlidogyrus sclerosus* Paperna and Thurston from cultured *Tilapia mossambica*. Kalikasan, Philipp. J. Biol. 2: 154-158.

Duncan, B.L. (1977). Urceolariid ciliates, including three new species, from cultured Philippine fishes. Trans. Amer. Microsc. Soc. 96:76-81.

Eldredge, L.G. (1994). Perspectives in aquatic exotic species management in the Pacific Islands. Volume 1: Introductions of commercially significant aquatic organisms to the Pacific Islands. South Pacific Commission, Noumea, New Caledonia, 127 p.

Foreign Trade Statistics of the Philippines (1990 to 1995). National Statistics Office, Manila, Philippines.

Galvez, E.R. (1979). Observations on the viability and resistance of the metacercaria of *Procerovum calderoni* (Africa and Garcia, 1935) Price, 1940 (Trematoda, Heterophyidae) in *Scatophagus argus* Linn. Fish. Res. J. Philipp. 4: 37-57.

Garcia, E.Y. (1936). Study on the resistance of the metacercaria of *Monorchotrema taihokui* to different physical chemical agents. J. Philipp. Isl. Med. Assoc. 16: 561-565.

Gindelberger, B.(1981). Fishery management in Camarines Sur. Why sinarapan almost disappeared from Lake Buhi. ICLARM Newsletter, 4(3): 3-5.

Infofish Fact Sheet. (1995). Infofish Fact Sheet. INFOFISH, Kuala Lumpur.

Jueco, N.L., Bobis, T.A. and Ramirez, L.M. (1971). Seasonal prevalence and density of *Anisakis* larvae in fishes (galunggong) sold in public markets in Manila. J. Philipp. Med. Assoc. 47: 467-476.

Juliano, R.O., Guerrero III, R. and Ronquillo, I. (1989). The introduction of exotic aquatic species in the Philippines. p. 83-90. *In* Exotic Aquatic Organisms in Asia. S.S. De Silva. (ed.) Asian Fisheries Society Special Publication 3. Asian Fisheries Society, Manila, Philippines.

Llobrera, A. (1987). Current fish disease problems in the Philippines and their economic impact. p. 22-28. *In* Fish Quarantine and Fish Diseases in South and Southeast Asia: 1986 Update. J.R. Arthur. (ed.) Report of the Asian Fish Health Network Workshop held in Manila, Philippines, May 30, 1986. Asian Fisheries Society Special Publication No. 1.

Lopez, N. (1986). Helminth and arthropod parasites of some freshwater fishes from Laguna Lake and vicinities. p. 19-20. *In* Fisheries Forum 1985-1986. Fisheries Research Department, PCARRD, Los Banos, Laguna.

Lumanlan, S.C, Albaladejo, J.D., Bondad-Reantaso, M.G. and Arthur, J.R. (1990). Freshwater fish imported into the Philippines: their parasite faunas and role in the international spread of parasitic diseases. p. 323-335. *In* Diseases in Asian Aquaculture I. M. Shariff, R.B. Subasinghe and J.R. Arthur. (eds.) Fish Health Section, Asian Fisheries Society, Manila, Philippines.

Macaranas, J.M., Taniguchi, N. Pante, M.J.R., Capili, J.B. and Pullin, R.S.V. (1986). Electrophoretic evidence for extensive hybrid gene introgression into commercial *Oreochromis niloticus* (L.) stocks in the Philippines. Aquaculture and Fisheries Management, 17: 249-358.

Mercene, E.C. (1995). Freshwater fishes of the Philippines. Paper presented at the First National Symposium Workshop on Aquatic Biology R & D, November 28-29, 1995. Lakeview Resort Hotel, Los Banos, Laguna. Sponsored by National Research Council of the Philippines, International Center for Living Aquatic Resources Management and Philippine Council for Marine and Aquatic Resources Development.

Natividad, J.M. (1987). Report on Philippine fish quarantine and certification programs. p. 62-72. *In* Fish Quarantine and Fish Diseases in South and Southeast Asia: 1986 Update. J.R. Arthur. (ed.) Report of the Asian Fish Health Network Meeting held in Manila, Philippines, 30 May 1986. Asian Fisheries Society Special Publication No. 1.

Natividad, J.M., Bondad-Reantaso, M.G. and Arthur, J.R. (1986). Parasites of Nile tilapia (*Oreochromis niloticus* (L.)) in the Philippines. p. 255-259. *In* The First Asian Fisheries Forum. J.L. Maclean, L.B. Dizon and L.V. Hosillos. (eds.) First Asian Fisheries Forum, Manila, Philippines, 26-31 May 1986. Asian Fisheries Society, Manila.

Philippine Fisheries Profile (1994). Bureau of Fisheries and Aquatic Resources, Manila.

Reantaso, M.B. (1991). EUS in brackishwaters of the Philippines. Asian Fisheries Society, Fish Health Section Newsletter, 2:8-9.

Refuerzo, P.G. (1940). Some helminths of dogs and cats transmissible to man in the Philippines with reference to their methods of transmission and prevention. Phillip. J. Animal Industry, 7: 493-524.

Regidor, S.E. and Arthur, J.R. (1986). Parasites of juvenile milkfish, Chanos chanos. p. 261-264. In The First Asian Fisheries Forum. J.L. Maclean, L.B. Dizon and L.V. Hosillos. (eds.) First Asian Fisheries Forum, Manila, Philippines, 26-31 May 1986. Asian Fisheries Society, Manila.

Soliman, V. (1994). Conservation and management of Lake Manapao (Philippines), a "sinarapan" (*Mistichthys luzoniensis*) sanctuary: status, problems and solutions. Mitt. International Verein Limnology, 24: 279-283.

Vasquez-Colet, A. (1943). The incidence of *Gnathostoma spinigerum* Owen in Philippine fish and Crustacea and its recovery in feeding experiments. Abstracts of Scientific Papers presented before the Conference on Medical Sciences in Commemoration of the Establishment of the Republic of the Philippines, December 20, 21 & 22, 1943, Manila. p. 75.(Abstract only).

Vasquez-Colet, A. and Africa, C.M. (1940). Morphological studies on various Philippine heterophyid metacercariae with notes on the incidence, site and degree of metacercarial infection in three species of marine fish. Phillip. J. Sci. 72: 395-419.

Velasquez, C.C. (1974). Ecological aspects of fish parasitology in the Philippines. p. 15-32. *In* Professorial Chair Lectures, Monograph 3, University of the Philippines Press, Quezon City.

Velasquez, C.C. (1975). Observations on the life cycle of *Carneophallus brevicaeca* (Africa and Garcia, 1935) comb. n. (Digenea: Microphallidae). J. Parasitol. 61: 910-914.

Velasquez, C.C. (1976). Some fish parasites as constraints of human welfare in the Philippines. p. 1-8. Professorial Chair Lectures, Monograph 22. University of the Philippines Press. Quezon City.

Velasquez, C.C. (1984). Pest/parasites and diseases of milkfish in the Philippines. p. 155-159. In Advances in Milkfish Biology and Culture. J.V. Juario, R.P. Ferraris and L.V. Benitz. (eds.) Island Publishing House, Metro Manila and SEAFDEC/AQD, Manila.

Table 1. Some information on ecological problems caused by introductions and transfers of aquatic organisms in the Philippines.

Species	Status	Reference
Glossogobius giurus	introduction to Lake Lanao island of Mindanao responsible for the depletion of endemic cyprinid population in the lake	Juliano et al. (1989)
Pomacea canaliculata (golden snail)	displacement of native snails (*Pila luzonica*; became a major pest in ricefields; extinction of one native species in Cagayan Valley	Acosta and Pullin (1991)
Poecilia latipinna (sailfin molly)	introduced for malarial mosquito control; became a pest in brackishwater	Juliano et al. (1989)
Oreochromis mossambicus	became a competitor for food in farms with *Chanos chanos*	Juliano et al. (1989)
Clarias batrachus	completely dominated the native freshwater catfish, *Clarias macrocephalus*	Juliano et al. (1989)
Tilapia	introduction of tilapia in lakes Buhi and Bato greatly reduced the population of 'sinarapan' (*Mistichthys luzonensis*)	Gindelberger (1980) Soliman (1993) Mercene (1995)
	introduction of tilapia in Taal Lake had a negative impact on the endemic freshwater sardine, *Sardinella tawilis*	Mercene (1995)

Table 2. List of exotic parasites which have become established in the Philippines (modified and updated from Natividad 1987).

Species	Hosts	Records
Trichodina centrostrigata Basson, Van As and Paperna, 1983	*Oreochromis niloticus*	Natividad et al. (1986) Bondad-Reantaso and Arthur (1989)
T. heterodentata Duncan, 1977	*O. mossambicus* *Tilapia zillii* *Trichogaster trichopterus*	Duncan (1977)
	O. niloticus	Natividad et al. (1986) Bondad-Reantaso and Arthur (1989)
	Cyprinus carpio	Albaladejo and Arthur (1989)
Trichodinella carpi Duncan, 1977	*Cyprinus carpio*	Duncan (1977) Paperna (1983) Albaladejo and Arthur (1989)
T. tilapiae Duncan, 1977	*T. zillii*	Duncan (1977)
Tripartiella clavodonta Basson and Van As, 1987	*O. niloticus*	Bondad-Reantaso and Arthur (1989)
Cichlidogyrus sclerosus Paperna and Thurston, 1969	*O. mossambicus* *O. niloticus* *O. niloticus*	Duncan (1973) Natividad et al. (1986) Bondad-Reantaso and Arthur (1990)
C. longicornis longicornis Paperna and Thurston, 1969	*O. niloticus*	Natividad et al. (1986) Bondad-Reantaso and Arthur (1990)
C. tiberianus Paperna, 1960	*O. niloticus*	Natividad et al. (1986) Bondad-Reantaso and Arthur (1990)

Table 2. Continued.

Species	Hosts	Records
C. tilapiae Paperna, 1960	*O. niloticus*	Natividad et al. (1986) Bondad-Reantaso and Arthur (1990)
Enterogyrus cichlidarum Paperna, 1963	*O. niloticus*	Bondad-Reantaso and Arthur (1990)
Gyrodactylus shariffi Cone, Arthur and Bondad-Reantaso, 1995	*O. niloticus*	Cone et al. (1995)
Bothriocephalus achielognathi Yamaguti, 1934	*Hypopthalmichthys nobilis* *Ctenopharyngodon idella* *Hypophthalmichthys molitrix*	Lumanlan et al. (1990)
	Glossogobius giurus	Lopez (1986)
Lernaea cyprinacea Linnaeus, 1758	*Chanos chanos*	Velasquez (1984) Regidor and Arthur (1986)
Cristaria plicata glochidium	*C. carpio* *O. niloticus*	Juliano et al. (1989) Bondad-Reantaso and Arthur (1990)

Table 3: Status of aquatic organisms introduced to the Pacific Islands from the Philippines (from Eldredge 1994).

Species	Country of destination	Year of introduction	Status
Fishes			
Neopomacantrus violascens	Guam	1989	Likely introduced by means of fouling or Navy barge hull towed to the Philippines or from ballast waters
Parioglossus sp.	Guam	June 1992	From the hull of a drydock towed from Subic Bay, Philippines
Omobranchus			
Parablennius thysanius	Hawaiian Is.	1971-1972	the Philippines ?
Oreochromis mossambicus	Guam	1954	for culture in tanks and brackishwater and for aquatic weed control
	Saipan	1955	to enhance stocks, impacts unknown
	New Caledonia	1955	for culture; well established
Oysters			
Crassostrea gigas	Fiji	1976	Cultured but no growth in 14 months
C. iredalei	Fiji	1975	About 300 specimens from Cavite, the Philippines, transported, all killed in flood 6 months later
Green mussel			
Perna viridis	Fiji	1975 (Apr)	800 specimens, initial mortality high; individuals surviving showed excellent growth; spawning twice a year
Perna viridis		1976 (Jan)	additional specimens, 99% survived during first 2 months

Table 3. Continued.

Species	Country of destination	Year of Introduction	Status
Perna viridis		1976	second introduction from the Philippines, initially grown at private farm until 1978
Perna viridis	Tonga	1975	transport attempted, no survival
Freshwater gastropods			
Pomacea lineata	Papua New Guinea		
Seaweeds			
Kappaphyncus cottoni	Kiribati	1977	
Eucheuma denticulatum	Kiribati	1977	
Gracilaria eucheumoides	Kaneohe Bay	mid-1970's	unknown success
Kappaphycus striatus	Honolulu Harbor	August 1970 to late 1976	successful
Gracilaria sp.	Honolulu	1971	unknown success
Kappaphycus alvarezzi	Honolulu Harbor	August 1974	successful

Table 4: Partial list of zoonotic parasites occurring in fresh and marine fishes in the Philippines

Disease/Host	Parasite	Reference
Nematode Disease		
a. Gnathostomiasis		
Glossogobius giurus	*Gnathostoma spinigerum*	Africa et al. (1936)
Ophicephalus striatus		Africa et al. (1937)
Therapon argenteus		Vasquez-Colet (1943)
Anabas testudineus		Velasquez (1974)
G. giurus		
O. striatus		
T. plumbeus		
b. Anisakiasis		
marine fishes	*Anisakis* sp.	Cabrera (1968)
marine fishes		Jueco et al. (1971)
c. Capillariasis		
Ambassis commersoni	*Capillaria philippinensis*	Cabrera et al. (1969)
Eleotris melanosoma		Cross et al. (1972)
Hypselotris bipartita		Cross et al. (1978)
d. Trichuriasis		
Eleotris melanosoma	*Trichuris sp.*	Cabrera et al. (1969)
Cestode Disease		
a. Diphyllobothriasis		
Eleotris melanosoma	*Diphyllobothrium* sp.	Cabrera et al. (1969)

Table 4. Continued.

Disease/Host	Parasite	Reference
Trematode Disease		
Anabas testudineus	*Procerovum calderoni*	Velasquez (1974)
	Stellantchasmus amplicaecalis	
	Centrocestus caninus	
G. giurus	*Centrocestus caninus*	Velasquez (1974)
T. plumbeus		
Arius manilensis	*Haplorchis yokogawai*	Africa (1937) Velasquez (1974)
Clarias batrachus		
O. striatus	*H. pumilio*	Refuerzo (1940)
		Velasquez (1974)
T. plumbeus		
Gerres filamentosus		Refuerzo (1940)
G. giurus		Refuerzo (1940) Velasquez (1974)
Puntius binotatus		Velasquez (1974)
Puntius binotatus	*H. taihokui*	Velasquez (1974)
Puntius palata		
Scatophagus argus	*Procerovum calderoni*	Galvez (1979)
G. giurus		Velasquez (1974)
O. striatus		

Table 4. Continued.

Disease/Host	Parasite	Reference
Ambassis buruensis	*P. calderoni*	Velasquez (1974)
	Stictodora guerreroi	
	S. manilensis	
	Heterophyopsis expectans	
O. striatus	*Clinostomum sp.*	Velasquez (1974)
Macrobrachium sp.	*Carneophallus brevicaeca*	Velasquez (1975)

Thailand

Pornlerd Chanratchakool

Aquatic Animal Health Research Institute
Kasetsart University Campus
Chatuchak, Bangkok 10900
Thailand

Abstract

Movement of live fish between Thailand and other countries for commercial purposes is an important trading activity. There is already a system for response to emergency fish disease outbreaks in the country, coordinated by the Department of Fisheries. A system for provision of health certificates is also in place. This paper describes the situation in Thailand and makes recommendations for future strengthening of quarantine and health certification.

Introduction

Movement of live fish between Thailand and other countries for commercial purposes has been reported since 1962. Almost all exported species of fish are for the ornamental/aquarium trade, with the U.S.A., EU and Japan and the main markets. This exporting business has grown very fast. From Thai Customs Department records, a total weight of 151 tonnes (valued at 12 million Baht[1]) was exported in 1978. In 1987, the total export value was 53 million Baht. This value is possibly lower than the actual export figure, with estimates from one large exporting company of around 480 million Baht in 1990.

The major importing market was United States, which imported around 40% of the total. Japan and the EU imported around 12.5% each. The remaining 35% was exported to Asian markets. Within Asia, the main markets are Singapore, Malaysia and Hong Kong, all of which act as "middle men" for re-export of fish to other markets. The average growth of the ornamental fish market was estimated around 5% per year. Apart from ornamental fish, white shrimp, frog, soft-shell turtle and freshwater prawn have also been exported to Hong Kong, China and Japan. From export figures, a very large volume of live aquatic organisms has been moving between countries, possibly becoming a potential vector for transferring aquatic animals diseases. Therefore, quarantine systems are required in each country in order to limit potential impacts caused by the spreading of aquatic animal pathogens and diseases.

International and in-country trade in aquatic organisms

In Thailand, around 100 species of fish are exported, of which 50% are wild fish. Fifteen species are cultured. The rest of them are imported species and successfully cultured within the country. Ornamental fish farms in Thailand are small and located in provinces near Bangkok, including Rachaburi, Nonthaburi, Supanburi, Nakhonsawan, Patumthani and Nakhonprathom. There are some farms in Bangkok where more expensive fish, such as discus, angelfish and oscar, are cultured. Wild or cultured fish are usually collected by local collectors or the exporting company. There are more than 30 exporting companies dealing with ornamental fish within the Bangkok area. The most common exported species are shown in Table 1.

Import statistics from the Thai Customs Department for 1988, show that 127 species of fish have been imported, with the major groups being catfish, carp, loach, tetra, bichir, arowana, gouramy, cichlid and rainbow. Almost all imported species are now cultured in Thailand for export. The Customs Department's records show that Thailand imported ornamental fish from eight countries including Singapore, Hong Kong, Japan, Germany, Malaysia, U.S.A., Sri Lanka and India.

The world total value of ornamental fish was estimated around 22,500 million Baht in 1992 (wholesale price) with a retail value of 75,000 million Baht. The three large markets are the U.S.A., the EC and Japan, who imported ornamental fish with a value of around 6,500 million Baht. Singapore and Hong Kong are the world's number 1 and number 2 exporting countries, with export values of 1,500 and 490 million Baht respectively. Thailand was number 3 exporter, with an export value of approximately 450 million Baht. However, some fish exported from Singapore and Hong Kong come from Thailand. (INFOFISH 1994). There are more than 30 exporting companies and these companies usually buy the fish from local collectors or local producers located near Bangkok. Eighty percent of the export species are wild fish whereas only 20% are cultured species (Wangchareonporn, 1991).

The collectors usually hold the fish in holding facilities and sell to the company, which sometimes exports fish directly. Sometimes, the exporters stock the fish at their own facilities before export. However, practices differ, depending on the supply, season and fish behavior. Most wild fish are usually exported directly from the local collector without holding at the exporting company.

Current status of aquatic animal quarantine and health certification programs

Aquatic animal diseases are one potential obstruction to trade. Trade issues related to aquatic animal diseases might be becoming more serious in many countries, such as the EU and Japan, as well as Australia. Some form of quarantine system has been established for many years in most importing countries in order to reduce risks associated with disease transfer through importing animals. In spite of this, there is evidence that some of new diseases and parasites have been spread from one country to another. To strengthen the existing quarantine system, requires collaboration between countries, involving both the government side and the private sector.

In Thailand, there are fisheries biologists working in the field all over the country. These government staff take care to report information on aquatic animal diseases through the Department of Fisheries (DoF) Fisheries Station or the Aquatic Animal Health Research Institute (AAHRI) directly. From time to time, DoF mobile units, located near fish and shrimp culture areas, also visit the farmer. Once a serious disease outbreak occurs, the DoF will announce and define the area to prevent the movement of diseased fish across the outbreak area. This approach has been used during EUS outbreaks in Thailand since 1980. In the absence of serious disease outbreaks, fish are allowed to be moved anywhere in the country.

Health certificates, issued by AAHRI, are required by most major importing countries, except Singapore. The certificates certify that the live fish are free from infectious pathogens, especially those that can be transferred from fish to fish.

To obtain a certificate, the exporter must submit the sample of fish along with the invoice to the authorized office for examination and issuance of the certificate. The authorized office is located near the point of export and near the border, such as in Phuket, Nong Kai, Songkhla and Chiang Mai. The sample for examination has to be in proportion of the export volume as follows:

- one percent of the specimens, if exporting more than 500 fish.
- three percent of the specimens, if exporting between 100-500 fish.
- five percent of the specimens, if exporting less than 100 fish.

The fish sample has to be submitted before exporting. The examination process requires 1-2 days before issuing the certificate. The certificate can be used within 7 days from the sample submission date.

For importing aquatic animal species into Thailand, there is no regulation on certification requirements from the Thai Government.

Problems

The export business for live aquatic animal is increasing very fast, particularly in the last two years. In 1994, around 500 certificates were issued from AAHRI; this increased to more than 1500 certificates in 1995. Many new companies are starting to export live aquatic organisms for human consumption, including, white shrimp, soft shell turtle, mantis shrimp, cockle, crab, frog and freshwater prawn. This exporting business is also growing very fast. A large quantity is being export almost every day. Health certificates are also required from importing countries such as Hong Kong, Japan, China and Korea. Since the animals are being used for human consumption, some countries require certification that the animals are free from human pathogens. However, such health certification requires time, 3-4 days, based on existing techniques and facilities available. In practice, it is sometimes difficult to hold animals in holding facilities for that long.

Since the Thai Government does not require a certificate for importing fish, this may be a possible route for introducing new disease to Thailand. There is some evidence that new diseases were transmitted from imported fish, such as *Lernaea* from Chinese carp, *Hexamita* from discus and *Edwardsiella ictaluri* from channel catfish.

Recommendations

Since many countries do not have a standard quarantine system, standardized procedures need to be established. Improving the existing systems to reach a standard acceptable to all countries may be required to ensure proper control. This approach would involve the following:

- Establishing practical guidelines for fish examination and issuing of health certificates.
- Exchange of disease information among the countries to restrict movement of fish out of areas affected by serious disease outbreaks.
- Increasing the number of authorized laboratories for issuing health certificates, as well as establishment of disease information centers.
- Training of staff and upgrading of laboratory facilities may needed in some countries.
- A regional working group should include strong representation from Asia.

References

INFOFISH (1994) The international trade in aquarium/ornamental fish. INFOFISH Internat. 5/94: 15-17

Wangchareonporn, W. (1991) Potential of ornamental fish breeding for export. Thai Fish. Gazette, 44: 171-174. (in Thai).

Table 1: Major exported fish species from Thailand.

Scientific name	Common name
Acantopsis choirorhynchos	Horseface loach
Pangio kuhlii	Coolie loach
Astronotus ocellatus	Oscar
Balantiocheilos melanopterus	Tricolor sharkminnow
Betta splendens	Siamese fighting fish
Botia modesta	Orangefin loach
Ctenopharyngodon idella	Grass carp
Dermogenys pusilla	Wrestling halfbeak
Crossocheilus oblongus	Siamese flying fox
Gyrinocheilus aymonieri	Siamese algae-eater
Gymnocorymbus ternetzi	Black tetra
Aristichthys nobilis	Bighead carp
Hypostomus sp.	Succer
Kryptopterus bicirrhis	Glass catfish
Epalzeorhynchos bicolor	Redtail sharkminnow
Epalzeorhynchos frenatum	Rainbow sharkminnow
Mastacembelus circumcinctus	Marble eel
Macrognathus aculeatus	Peacock eel
Labeo chrysophekadion	Black sharkminnow
Pangasius sutchi	Sutchi catfish
Pangasius larnaudii	Spot pangasius
Puntius tetrazona	Sumatra barb
Barbodes schwanenfeldii	Goldfoil barb
Rasbora heteromorpha	Harlequin rasbora
Rasbora trilineata	Three-lined rasbora
Scatophagus argus	Spotted scat
Symphysodon discus	Red discus
Trichogaster lalia	Dwarf gourami

ANNEX VI: GENERAL PRINCIPLES FOR REGIONAL QUARANTINE

The following general principles for regional aquatic animal quarantine measures were discussed during the workshop.

1. Trade in living aquatic animals and aquatic animal products is economically and socially justifiable. An entitlement exists within and between nations for individuals or organizations to import such animals or products where deleterious effects can be minimized or avoided. Considerable benefits have resulted from the introduction of aquatic animals and aquatic animal products.

2. Living aquatic animals and aquatic animal products imported for different purposes should be treated in a similar manner where equal risk of introducing exotic disease exists, i.e., an equity of principle must apply in all considerations.

3. Concerns regarding exotic disease incursions and concerns regarding adverse environmental impacts are inexorably linked with imports of living aquatic animals: Both issues must be addressed in considering such imports, but exotic disease and pest exclusion should be treated as a separate function of quarantine.

4. Quarantine should operate from the basic axiom that any importation of living aquatic animals or products derived therefrom should be allowed entry unless they pose an unacceptable level of disease risk to national fisheries resources and the environment.

5. A conservative approach should be adopted in cases where insufficient knowledge exists in relation to disease risks posed by a particular import; A higher stringency of quarantine should be adopted where inadequate knowledge exists.

6. Particular countries or regions may enjoy a privileged position with regard to freedom from exotic pathogens and parasites of aquatic animals and greater levels of quarantine stringency may reasonably be imposed by those countries or regions to protect the status quo than might otherwise be indicated.

7. The likelihood of an exotic agent establishing in susceptible endemic hosts in the aquatic environment of the importing country should be regarded as a major consideration on which to base quarantine assessments.

8. Imports should be considered on an individual basis with quarantine commensurate with risks, considering source and destination of the import.

9. Individual countries may need to adopt, modify or vary guidelines to suit their own particular purposes: A minimum standard of quarantine should apply.

10. Quarantine should not be used as a non-tariff trade barrier. Valid disease concerns must be present in order to justify imposition of quarantine procedures.

11. Quarantine should serve to protect the natural environment and natural aquatic fauna, as well as serve to support and protect trade in aquatic animal species.

12. As far as possible, regional countries should attempt to harmonize aquatic animal health certification and quarantine practices and procedures to facilitate movements and introductions of aquatic animals and aquatic animal products.

ANNEX VII: STRATEGY FOR THE DEVELOPMENT AND IMPLEMENTATION OF HEALTH CERTIFICATION AND QUARANTINE GUIDELINES FOR THE RESPONSIBLE MOVEMENT OF AQUATIC ANIMALS IN THE ASIA-PACIFIC REGION

Background

The production of food through aquaculture and trade in aquatic animals and their products constitutes an activity of major economic and social importance to the Asian region. The total aquaculture production in Asia has grown from 3.7 million tonnes in 1976 to 25.46 million tonnes in 1994, representing more than 89% of the total world aquaculture production1, with an estimated value of US$ 39.8 billion.

However, disease outbreaks are also becoming economically and socially significant constraints to aquaculture production and trade in many countries of the region. For example, the economic loss attributed to outbreaks of disease in developing countries of the Asia-Pacific Region was estimated to be at least US$ 1.4 billion in 1990 alone2. Since 1990, this serious aquatic disease situation in the region has deteriorated. Furthermore, the economic loss from shrimp farms in China in 1993 was more than US$ 1 billion 3. Recent estimates, based on farm level surveys in 16 Asian countries, indicate that disease and environment-related problems may cause annual losses to aquaculture production in Asian countries of more than US$ 3 billion per year (ADB/NACA, 1996). Apart from the economic impacts on aquaculture industries, pathogen transfer and disease can have significant, although generally poorly quantified, impacts on aquatic biological diversity ranging from alteration of population genetic structure to distribution of a species in the changing community structure.

It is widely recognized that improved regulatory and technical measures are necessary to prevent the introduction and spread of diseases and pests to protect industries based on aquaculture and to protect the aquatic environment from the adverse effects of such diseases or pests. Uniform practices and procedures designed to prevent introductions of diseases or pests which are applicable to a particular region should support and protect aquaculture whilst minimizing impediments to trade.

The Articles 9.3.2 and 9.3.3 of the Code of Conduct on Responsible Fisheries which was agreed upon and approved by the FAO member countries at the

---

1 Based on FAO fisheries statistics, estimates for global aquaculture production in 1994 are 25.46 million tonnes with an estimated total value of US$ 39.83 billion.

2 Source: RETA 5358: Regional Study and Workshop on Fish Disease and Fish Health Management (ADB/NACA, 1991)

3 The annual production from Chinese shrimp farms declined from 219 ,571 tonnes in 1991 to 63,872 tonnes in 1994.

twenty-eighth Session of the FAO Conference (20 October to 2 November 1995, Rome) respectively state that "States should cooperate in the elaboration, adoption and implementation of international codes of practice and procedures for introductions and transfers of aquatic organisms" and "States should, in order to minimize risks of disease transfer and other adverse effects on wild and cultured stocks, encourage adoption of appropriate practices in the genetic improvement of broodstocks, the introduction of non-native species, and in the production, sale and transport of eggs, larvae or fry, broodstock or other live materials. States should facilitate the preparation and implementation of appropriate national codes of practice and procedures to this effect" (FAO, 1995). In order to facilitate development of national codes of practice on health certification and quarantine for aquatic animals and animal products, as a response to the requests made by the FAO member countries, the Fisheries Department of FAO embarked upon an activity to develop a global document on practical guidelines for the responsible movement (introduction and transfer) of aquatic organisms.

The regional importance of aquatic animal health management and the need for aquatic animal quarantine have been recognized by the Network of Aquaculture Centres in Asia and the Pacific (NACA), and a program to develop and implement aquatic animal health management has been incorporated into the second five year work program of NACA (NACA, 1996). At the request of member countries, NACA Governing Council has recommended the drafting and adoption of regional guidelines for health certification and quarantine of aquatic animals in the Asia-Pacific region.

The concept of, and need for, regional aquatic animal quarantine has been promoted at a number of expert meetings and workshops over the past two decades. Such meetings and workshops have generally made recommendations pertaining to the need for quarantine and the human and physical research capability necessary to support health certification and disease testing programs. Responding to needs for the development and adoption of minimum aquatic animal health certification and quarantine guidelines for the region, FAO in collaboration with NACA and the Aquatic Animal Health Research Institute in Thailand (AAHRI), a recognized regional center of excellence in aquatic animal health management, convened a Regional Workshop on Health and Quarantine Guidelines for the Responsible Movement (Introduction and Transfer) of Aquatic Organisms in January 1996 in Bangkok, Thailand. The purpose of this workshop was to develop a strategy for a cooperative framework involving key fisheries and veterinary authorities in regional countries that may be used to implement adoption of uniform regional quarantine practices. The workshop was attended by participants from countries of the region, and representatives from a number of regional and international institutions including FAO, NACA, Office International des Epizooties (OIE), Australian Center for International Agricultural Research (ACIAR), Asian Fisheries Society and AAHRI.

This summary document describes the key features of the strategy developed and agreed upon by the participants of the workshop.

Objectives

The main objective of the strategy is to develop practical and effective regional and national health certification and quarantine guidelines which minimize the negative impact of aquatic animal diseases on aquaculture, inland and coastal fisheries, and indigenous aquatic biological diversity. In doing so, the strategy addresses the need for countries to develop practical and enforceable measures to reduce risks associated with the introduction of aquatic animal pathogens. At the present time, several countries are in the process of establishing or considering the establishment of quarantine facilities and other procedures to reduce risks associated with the introduction of aquatic animal pathogens. This is largely in response to the serious economic damage to the aquaculture sector caused by recent outbreaks of fish and shrimp disease in countries of the Asian region.

Facilitating agencies

NACA would be the coordinating and implementing agency for the proposed strategy and would be the primary focus for communication with regional and international bodies and groups in relation to development of health certification and quarantine procedures. FAO will closely collaborate with NACA in the development of health certification and quarantine guidelines and would advise and assist NACA in implementing the overall strategy. The Fish Diseases Commission of OIE, the South Pacific Commission (SPC), AAHRI and ACIAR would also support the implementation of the strategy and provide advice and assistance to NACA.

Mechanism

The proposed strategy consists of three phases. Phase I: collection and analysis of Asia regional epidemiological data, Phase II: formulation and ratification of guidelines, and Phase III: implementation, monitoring, evaluation and revision of guidelines. Ten activities have been identified within the first two phases of the strategy. The activities of the third phase will be determined on the basis of the experience and knowledge gained, and progress made during Phases I and II.

Phase I: Collection and Analysis of Asia Regional Fish Health Data

- **Activity 1: Appointment of National Coordinators**

Each participating country would appoint a National Coordinator who would be responsible for the collection, collation and dissemination of information related to fish disease and fish health management. As the development of national quarantine system requires inputs from different technical and legal agencies and the private sector, the possibility of developing national quarantine committees will be explored.

Initially the regional governments should be represented through national coordinators, and increasing communication, collaboration and liaison would be developed and maintained with the governments through NACA co-ordination and by direct liaison with individuals or committees in each country nominated for this purpose.

Time Frame: Participating countries have been approached by NACA to appoint National Coordinators.

- **Activity 2 : Establishment of a Regional Working Group (RWG)**

The Regional Working Group (RWG) on Aquatic Animal Health Certification and Quarantine will be formed as a starting point to initiate the drafting of guidelines. The RWG would be responsible for liaison with all parties involved and for the ongoing development, circulation, revision and promotion of regional aquatic animal health certification and quarantine guidelines. The RWG would also assume a role in collation of disease data and compilation of current quarantine policies and practices. The data collected by the National Coordinators will be analyzed by the RWG for the formulation of draft guidelines. The secretariat of the RWG group will be based in NACA.

Involvement of the aquafarming sector from the early phase of implementation is considered essential for the success of the strategy. Therefore, the farming sector will be represented at the RWG through inducting an appropriate person from the sector. The industry views and opinions will be considered in developing and implementing the strategy.

As an initiating step for implementing the strategy, and before any attempts are made to develop and circulate draft guidelines, consultation with individual countries is an essential pre-requisite. Such consultation would determine each country's thoughts regarding regional aquatic animal health certification and quarantine and their respective needs and problems, and how these needs and problems are best approached.

Composition. The RWG should comprise a small group (6-8) of individuals with wide experience and expertise in aquatic animal health certification and quarantine matters. The RWG will use the services of other specialists as necessary.

Resources. Members of the RWG would require access to computing, secretarial and information technology services and should have close contacts with government and non-governmental organizations and individuals within the Asia- Pacific Region and elsewhere.

Time Frame: NACA will prepare a list of potential RWG members and forward it to FAO for consideration and short listing. The list of RWG members will be available by <u>November 1997</u>.

- **Activity 3 : Development of a Computer - based Fish Health Data Collection System**

FAO will develop a computer-based data collection system for aquatic animal health including diseases and pathogens, which will be used to facilitate the collection and exchange of information relevant to the countries of the region.

Time Frame: This activity is also underway and a functional prototype of the database will be developed by May 1997. A pilot data set, will be fed into the database during its development. The database may require adoption to suit the geo-political differences in different countries in the region. Such changes would be identified during the initial consultation between the RWG and National Coordinators planned for January 1998 (Activity 4).

- **Activity 4 : Initial Consultation between RWG and National Coordinators**

An initial meeting between the RWG and National Coordinators is recommended to identify specific needs on aquatic animal health data for the formulation of guidelines, and also for establishing the database on regional fish health. This initial meeting would also discuss matters to finalize the logistics and criteria for regional data collection, collation, analysis and preparation of guidelines. This initial meeting will also help to amend the modules of the database to include geo-political differences in the regional countries, and also to harmonize the data collection procedures.

Time Frame: January 1998

- **Activity 5 : Collection of Regional Fish Health Data**

The National Coordinators will co-ordinate collection of information from the countries of the region using the computer-based data collection system that would be deployed by FAO. A group of 13 fish disease specialists from 8 countries in the region have attended a " Master Class on Epidemiology in Tropical Aquaculture" organized by ACIAR during July 1996. The trainees of the "Master Class" will act as national resource persons and help conducting training for data collectors in their own country. Bibliographic data collected and compiled by the Fish Health Section of the Asian Fisheries Society will also be used to supplement the database. Data available through previous and ongoing fish health exercises of FAO, NACA, AAHRI and ACIAR will also be utilized for this purpose. It is expected that by the end of this activity adequate fish health/epidemiological data from the region will be available for analysis.

Time Frame: Data collection will start from January 1998

Phase II : Formulation and Ratification of Guidelines.

- **Activity 6 : Establishment of an *ad hoc* Advisory Committee (AC)**

An *ad hoc* advisory committee (AC) would be established to facilitate the dissemination and exchange of information on global issues related to aquatic animal health certification and quarantine. The role of the group within the proposed strategy would be basically advisory and facilitatory. The committee would be comprised of assigned officers from FAO and OIE (Fish Disease Commission in particular), and would invite representatives from other concerned agencies to participate as and when required.

Time Frame : This ad hoc committee will be in place during 1998.

- **Activity 7 : Appointment of an Aquatic Animal Health Specialist to NACA**

A key component of the strategy is the appointment of an aquatic animal health specialist to NACA. This person would work within NACA and be responsible for liaison between the RWG, AC, and other concerned agencies, and would also co-ordinate the implementation of the regional strategy. NACA Governing Council has agreed to create a position for an aquatic animal health specialist.

Time Frame: It is envisaged that a suitable person would be appointed soon. Until such a person is appointed, NACA has placed an experienced Senior Aquaculturist who has a good background in fish diseases.

- **Activity 8 : Regional Workshop on Aquatic Animal Health Certification and Quarantine**

A major regional workshop to introduce the concept of regional aquatic animal health certification and quarantine is envisaged, with the opportunity for each regional country to present issues, problems and needs relating to certification and quarantine. Representation and involvement of industry groups at such a workshop may assist in eliciting awareness and support for the strategy. The workshop will introduce the concepts, principles and available information on regional aquatic animal health certification and quarantine so far collected and prepared by the RWG to the participants. It would also include discussion of known incursions of disease associated with introduction and transfers of aquatic animals and aquatic animal products and the social, economic and environmental costs (including biodiversity impacts) of such incursions. Participants will be requested to present status reports on aquatic animal health certification and quarantine in their respective countries. A clear objective of the workshop would be to assist the drafting of minimal aquatic animal health certification and quarantine guidelines.

Time Frame: The workshop, with attending representatives from all participating countries, members of the AC and RWG, and other interested parties, is proposed to be held in December 1998.

- **Activity 9 : Drafting, Distribution, and Revision of Guidelines**

The draft guidelines first compiled by the RWG will be circulated to all interested parties for comment. The parties will include all governments, industry and trade groups, interest groups, research organizations, and other concerned groups and agencies. All individuals, organizations, industries, and academic institutions which may have a role or that may be impacted upon by changes to quarantine procedures should be given the opportunity to comment.

It is emphasized that the guidelines are in no way intended to subvert, replace or restrict the legislation of individual countries with respect to quarantine. It is clear that individual countries will maintain the right to formulate and implement their own legislation. The guidelines are intended to assist in this process.

All comments and suggestions made by all parties will be addressed in a revised draft of the document (second draft) which will be compiled by the RWG. A register of replies and comments should be maintained and appended to the document. All parties will again distribute revised copies of guidelines for consideration. Special attention will be paid to ensuring that comments by respondents have been addressed.

Time Frame: The draft guidelines (second draft) are expected to be ready by July 1999. They will be circulated in August 1999.

- **Activity 10 : Adoption in Principle of the Guidelines**

A major regional conference specifically to discuss the revised minimal health certification and quarantine guidelines (second draft) involving all interested parties, especially representatives from all key agencies and departments of regional countries, will be held. The agenda for the meeting will be clearly spelt out, i.e., that the meeting is to seek formal agreement and adoption in principle of the minimal quarantine guidelines by those government representatives present.

Representatives should be clear that acceptance and adoption of the minimal guidelines at the meeting does not constitute adoption by their respective governments. Rather, it is adoption in principle by regional experts and authorities of the principles. Following satisfactory collaboration and revision, formal ratification and adoption in principle of the guidelines by members of regional countries are necessary.

Time Frame : The meeting is to be held in September 1999.

Phase III: Implementation, monitoring and appropriate revision of guidelines.

The ultimate objective of the strategy is that guidelines for appropriate regional aquatic animal health and quarantine be embodied in the legislation of regional countries such that a regional uniformity exists. This does not mean that each country should have the same legislation. Rather, individual legislation should provide for common practices and uniformity to facilitate regional trade and movement of aquatic animals and aquatic animal products.

Once the guidelines are formally agreed upon and adopted in principle, they need to be translated to individual country legislation. This is left to the individual countries and, if requested by the countries, the AC and RWG will provide assistance and support to do so.

It is imperative that the occurrence of aquatic animal diseases and development of health certification and quarantine procedures by the individual countries be monitored so that necessary amendments/ revisions to the guidelines could be formulated. Thus, it is proposed that the AC and RWG will continue to meet at two-year intervals to evaluate the regional status with respect to aquatic animal health certification and quarantine.

The details of the activities involved in this phase would be formulated on the basis of experience and knowledge gained, and progress made during Phases I and II.

ANNEX VIII: A BRIEF REVIEW OF HEALTH CERTIFICATION AND QUARANTINE CODES AND GUIDELINES, AND THEIR PRACTICAL APPLICABILITY TO THE ASIA-PACIFIC REGION

Introduction

International, national and regional legislation, policies, practices and guidelines relating to quarantine and health certification for the introduction and translocation of living aquatic animals and their products are in a state of constant change. Frequent revision and modification are necessitated by rapid world-wide developments in aquaculture and capture fisheries, rapidly increasing knowledge on diseases of aquatic animals, and improved or new diagnostic tests and procedures. Further, the changing political, social, ecological, industrial and economic environments of individual countries and regions which are increasingly responsive to changing trade practices, disease distribution patterns and risk assessments have contributed to this current global dynamic state of aquatic animal quarantine and health certification.

As an adjunct to national quarantine legislation and policies, guidelines and codes of practice have been developed, modified and revised by international agencies or working groups vested with responsibilities for animal disease control. These codes and guidelines have been developed in part to provide a level of international uniformity and standardization for the prevention of disease transfers associated with the importation, exportation and within country movement of living aquatic animals. They include:

- The Office International des Epizooties (OIE) Aquatic Animal Health Code (OIE 1995);
- The ICES Code of Practice on the Introductions and Transfers of Marine Organisms, 1994 (ICES 1995), and its earlier versions.
- The International Council for Exploration of the Sea (ICES) and the European Inland Fisheries Advisory Commission (EIFAC) Codes of Practice and Manual of Procedures for Consideration of Introductions and Transfers of Marine and Freshwater Organisms (Turner 1988);
- The ICES Guidelines for the Implementation of the ICES Code of Practice Concerning Introductions and Transfers of Marine Species (ICES 1984); and
- The ICES Overview of Current Molluscan Disease Control Measures (ICES 1991)

In general, there are as many differing sets of quarantine practices and procedures as there are individual countries. As noted, policies are frequently under revision, considerable variations occur between countries and little uniformity exists. Some countries have highly restrictive practices designed to ensure importation of aquatic animals free from specific pathogens; others have quarantine legislation which is inadequately enforced; others still have no restrictions or quarantine requirements.

In preventing the international spread of aquatic animal disease, the onus remains upon each importing country to establish its own requirements for aquatic animal quarantine, taking into account the enzootic disease status, the need to protect fisheries resources from exotic disease incursions and the need to maintain export markets based on healthy stocks of fish and aquatic invertebrates. Most countries, therefore, specify at least minimal quarantine or certification requirements for certain species of fish or eggs.

The nature, diversity, inconsistency and incompatibility of current quarantine procedures worldwide are reviewed by Humphrey (1995). Quarantine for fish generally follows three strategies, which may be used separately or in combination: certification of production facilities, shipment inspection and quarantine, which may occur prior to or after shipment, or both. In countries where quarantine, disease testing and accreditation procedures can be relied upon, farm certification may be a satisfactory means of importing specific pathogen-free stocks. In other cases, especially in tropical and subtropical regions, where the number of fish species imported and exported is large, knowledge of fish diseases incomplete and disease testing facilities limited or absent, it is doubtful that a system of on-farm inspection and certification could work.

The European Community (EC) is an exception. European Community Council Regulations have established the health conditions governing placing on the market of cultured aquatic animals and their products (Council of the European Communities 1991, De Kinkelin and Hedrick 1991). Member countries must abide by such directives.

The OIE Aquatic Animal Health Code

The Office International des Epizooties (OIE), an international veterinary organization with 139 member countries, has recently developed revised recommendations and protocols for the prevention of the international spread of diseases of fish, molluscs and crustaceans given in its International Aquatic Animal Health Code (OIE 1995).

The objective of the OIE Code is to facilitate international trade in aquatic animal species and their products, and it is intended to provide the veterinary administrations of member countries with guidelines for the trade in living and dead aquatic animals (De Kinkelin and Hedrick 1991). It is written primarily for aquatic animal species of socio-economic importance, and consequently specifies diseases of those species which are of concern to member countries.

The Code contains chapters on certification and inspection procedures, transport, disinfection, communications, and model certificates. It provides detailed definitions of minimum health guarantees required of trading partners to avoid risk of spreading aquatic animal disease, based on inspection by a competent authority, epizootilogical surveillance, use of standard methods for laboratory examinations and disease diagnosis, and a system of disease-free and infected zones for a range of important diseases. The Code also stresses the need for certification as a pre-requisite for controlling and preventing the international spread of aquatic animal diseases and provides a list of "Diseases Notifiable to the OIE" and a list of "Other Significant Diseases." exchange.

In its introductory chapters, the Code:

- Provides detailed definitions of minimum health guarantees required of trading partners to avoid risk of spreading aquatic animal diseases, based on inspection by a competent authority, epizootilogical surveillance, and standard methods for laboratory examinations and disease diagnosis.
- Stresses the need for certification as a pre-requisite for controlling and preventing the international spread of aquatic animal diseases.
- Emphasizes that certification should be a means of facilitating trade and not an impediment to such.
- Notes that under the Code, certification is generally required for all diseases notifiable to OIE.
- In regard to certification, the Code:
- Stresses the need for certification to be simple and unambiguous, and provides model certificates for this purpose.
- Suggests that all certificates be officially stamped, signed and validated to prevent forgery, inappropriate or multiple use of the same document.
- Emphasizes that no person or competent authority should sign health certification forms for matters for which they have not directly been responsible, unless supported by ancillary facts or evidence.
- Details the principles of certification requirements.
- Stresses the need for the definition and determination of a competent authority for export/import purposes by bilateral consultation between the countries involved, the circumstances for competency being appropriate to specific circumstances.

In regard to communications between OIE and member countries, the Code specifies reporting and notification arrangements and requirements of member countries, including a requirement for notification of occurrences or suspect occurrences of diseases notifiable to OIE or other significant disease events.

The Code also:

- Provides an overview of import risk analysis, emphasizing the importance of the numerical quantity of product or species to be imported; the occurrence and prevalence of disease in the exporting country or zone; and the levels of disease surveillance and environmental, processing or other factors which will mitigate against survival of pathogens.
- Provides guidelines for transport of aquatic animals, with provisions for prevention of spillage, disinfection of containers and treatment of transport water.
- Specifies health measures to be applied prior to, during and after transit, including a requirement for identification and inspection of the consignment of living or dead animals by a competent authority; a possible need for implementation of pre-export tests specified by the importing country; transport under secure conditions; notification of the importing country in the event of a notifiable disease outbreak in the premises of origin after export; health and laboratory examinations by a competent authority; establishment of "frontier posts" for receipt and initial handling and inspection of animals and provision for disinfection and disposal of potentially contaminated materials; and minimal health measures upon importation.
- Strongly promotes the concept of allowing entry of animals or products from a zone or country of equivalent or better disease status relative to the country or zone in the importing country for the disease in question.
- Provides brief guidelines for the transfer of biological and pathogenic agents and gives details on methods for destruction of pathogens and disinfection procedures.

The Code provides a list of "Diseases Notifiable to the OIE" and a list of "Other Significant Diseases." "Diseases Notifiable to the OIE" are generally regarded as having the potential for serious damage to national aquaculture industries or to wild populations of fish, molluscs or crustaceans. "Other Significant Diseases" include those diseases which are serious but have a broad geographic distribution; those causing significant mortality, transmissible, and of limited geographic range, but for which the etiological agent has not yet been identified; and those diseases with potential for causing large losses, but which are too new for their geographic range to be defined or for essential epidemiological elements to be understood.

The Code makes provision for elevation of significant diseases to notifiable status, and for diseases to be removed. Considerable attention is directed to establishing criteria for the definition of disease-free and infected zones with respect to diseases notifiable to OIE within individual countries. In this regard, the Code:

- Notes that a country may be free of the disease.
- Specifies three types of zones: disease-free zone; surveillance zone and; infected zone.
- Provides for disease-free aquaculture establishments
- Provides for the restoration of free status.
- Emphasizes the need for a country to demonstrate a reliable system of disease control and surveillance, that diseases are legally notifiable and that an effective organization for disease control in aquaculture establishments must exist in order that a country may be recognized as disease free.

For the purposes of the Code, a country is considered free from a specified disease when no recorded outbreak of the disease has occurred within its territory for at least the previous two years, or when the disease or pathogen has not been detected in any fish, mollusc or crustacean tested during the operation of a national health surveillance scheme, using the procedures described in the OIE Diagnostic Manual for Aquatic Animal Diseases.

For fish, a disease-free zone within a country may be part of the territory or country where the agent is present, but such a zone can only compromise aquaculture establishments and wild populations which have been tested in an official fish health surveillance scheme for at least the previous two years, using the procedures described in the OIE manual, and in which the pathogen has not been detected during the two-year period. Such disease free zones must comprise one or more entire water catchment areas from the sources of the waterway to the sea, or part of a catchment area from the source(s) to a natural or artificial barrier which prevents the upward migration of fish from lower stretches of the waterway. Such zones must be clearly delineated on a map of the territory of the country concerned by the Competent Authority.

For molluscs, a disease-free zone is defined by the Code as a well-defined part of the coastal territory of a country, as defined by the Competent Authorities, in which fishing and/or mollusc farming takes place. The area covered by the zone is based on evidence from maritime traditions, hydrographic characteristics and geographical features. Such zones must be clearly delineated on a map of the territory or country by the Competent

Authority. A zone of a country may be considered free from a molluscan disease when the agent has never been detected under the conditions defined under free country.

A disease-free aquaculture establishment for fish or molluscs may be located not only within a disease-free country or zone, but also within an infected zone, provided that:

- It has been tested in an official fish health surveillance scheme for at least the previous two years, using the procedures described in the OIE Manual, without the detection of the pathogen.
- In the case of fish, it is supplied with water only from a spring, well or borehole and free of stocks of wild fish. In the case of molluscs, it is supplied with water by a means which ensures removal or destruction of the pathogen present.
- There is a natural or artificial barrier which prevents the migration of fish from lower stretches of the waterway into the farm or its water supply.

For the classification of country, zone and establishment freedom, the country must observe OIE conditions relating to the provision by the appropriate competent authorities of an international aquatic animal health certificate for imports of living fish, sexual products and dead fish; and that living fish or sexual products shall only be moved into zones of equivalent status.

A country, zone or an aquaculture establishment may be restored to disease-free status if the pathogen has not been detected for the last two years of a surveillance scheme using the procedures described in the OIE manual.

In relation to Other Significant Diseases, the Code advises that when importing living or killed susceptible species, that the competent authority of the importing country may wish to require the presentation of a health certificate from the competent authority on the exporting country attesting that the site of origin has been regularly tested and/or freedom from the disease at the site of origin of the species. With certain diseases, visual examination and freedom from clinical signs or evidence of disease on the day of shipment is required. The Code does not nominate Other Significant Diseases of molluscs.

The pathogens, parasites and diseases specified in OIE Aquatic Animal Health Code are as follows:

Diseases Notifiable to OIE

a. Diseases of Fish

- Epizootic haematopoietic necrosis
- Infectious haematopoietic necrosis
- Oncorhynchus masou virus disease
- Spring viraemia of carp
- Viral haemorrhagic septicaemia

b. Diseases of Molluscs

- Bonamiosis (*Bonamia ostreae*, *Bonamia* sp.)
- Haplosporidiosis (*Haplosporidium nelsoni*)
- Marteiliosis (*Marteilia refringens*, *M. sydneyi*)
- Mikrocytosis (*Mikrocytos roughleyi*, *M. mackini*)
- Perkinsosis (*Perkinsus atlanticus*, *P. marinus*, *P. olseni*)
- Iridovirosis (iridovirus)

Other Significant Diseases

a. Diseases of Fish

- Channel catfish virus disease
- Viral encephalopathy and retinopathy
- Infectious pancreatic necrosis
- Infectious salmon anemia
- Epizootic ulcerative syndrome
- Bacterial kidney disease (*Renibacterium salmoninarum*)
- Enteric septicemia of catfish (*Edwardsiella ictaluri*)
- Piscirickettsiosis (*Piscirickettsia salmoninarum*)

b. Diseases of Crustaceans

- Baculoviral midgut gland necrosis
- Nuclear polyhedrosis baculoviroses (Penaeus monodon-type baculovirus, *Baculovirus penaei*)

- Infectious hypodermal and hematopoietic necrosis virus
- Yellowhead disease
- Crayfish plague (*Aphanomyces astaci*)

Originally, the Aquatic Animal Health Code was intended as guidelines, not as a global document governing international trade. However, as part of the General Agreement on Tariff and Trade (GATT), the accepted international standards governing the movement of animals are those of OIE. The International Aquatic Animal Health Code has thus assumed greater importance than originally intended because of the GATT agreement. These rules would govern international trade in aquatic animals; countries placing restrictions on trade outside of the Code could face protests to the World Trade Organisation (WTO) under the agreement. In general, countries could not apply standards higher than those specified by the Code. If any country wished to apply more stringent measures, then a risk assessment would have to be undertaken to justify additional measures.

It is envisaged that the Code will be subject to a continual process of refinement and updating. It is also generally accepted that the Code does not apply well in developing countries. Responsibilities for reporting disease occurrences to OIE rest with the veterinary administration of member countries. In Asia-Pacific region, however, veterinarians are often less involved in aquatic animal health than are the various national fishery departments. As official channels of communication with OIE are through the Chief Veterinary Officer of each member country, it is not surprising that OIE receives little or no information on aquatic animal diseases from Asia-Pacific countries. A need to better organize the communication channels for fish disease information to OIE exists. Further, communications should be opened between veterinary and fisheries departments to facilitate information.

The ICES Code of Practice on the Introductions and Transfers of Marine Organisms

The International Council for the Exploration of the Sea (ICES), through its Working Group on Introductions and Transfers of Marine Organisms and through cooperation with other ICES Working Groups and with the European Inland Fisheries Advisory Commission (EIFAC) of the UNFAO, has developed a Code of Practice to address potential problems resulting from the introduction or transfer of non-native marine organisms for fisheries enhancement and mariculture purposes. These potential problems include the inadvertent coincident movement of harmful organisms (including disease agents) associated with the target (host) species, potential ecological and environmental impacts of introduced and transferred species, and possible genetic impacts due to the mixing of farmed and wild stocks and the release of genetically modified organisms (ICES 1995).

The Code was first adopted on 10 October, 1973 (ICES 1995), and a revised Code, subsequently adopted in October 1979, became the standard for international policy and the version of the Code most widely used, cited and translated for the next 10 years. Minor revisions and additions led to the adoption in October 1990 of a "1990 Revised Code". The most recent version of the Code, the "ICES Code of Practice on the Introductions and Transfers of Marine Organisms, 1994," was adopted by ICES in September 1994. It incorporates further changes and adds new sections relative to genetic issues.

A number of related documents have been published by ICES and the European Inland Fisheries Advisory Commission, most notably two extended guides to the Code, the "Guidelines for Implementing the ICES Code of Practice Concerning Introductions and Transfers of Marine Species' (ICES 1984) and the "Codes of Practice and Manual of Procedures for Consideration of Introductions and Transfers of Marine and Freshwater Organisms" (Turner 1988). These guides are currently under revision by the ICES Working Group on Introductions and Transfers of Marine Organisms (ICES 1995). Additional relevant ICES documents include the "Overview of Current Molluscan Disease Control Measures" (ICES 1991) and the various annual reports of the Working Group on Introductions and Transfers of Marine Organisms.

The ICES Code of Practice on the Introductions and Transfers of Marine Organisms, 1994

The ICES Code of Practice provides recommendations for dealing with new intentional introductions of marine and brackishwater organisms, and procedures for species which are part of existing commercial practice to reduce the risks of detrimental effects resulting from these translocations. The Code is aimed at a broad audience, which includes governmental, commercial and private (including scientific) interests.

The Code is divided into five sections of recommendations:

a) Section I provides a recommended procedure for all species prior to reaching a decision regarding new introductions.

b) Section II outlines recommended actions if the decision is taken to proceed with the introduction. The recommended procedure, which includes quarantine and inspection, is as follows:

- A broodstock should be established in a quarantine situation approved by the country of receipt, in sufficient time to allow adequate evaluation of the stock's health status.

- The first generation progeny of the introduced species can be transplanted to the natural environment if no disease agents or parasites become evident in the first generation progeny, but not the original import. In the case of fish, broodstock should be developed from stocks imported as eggs or juveniles, to allow sufficient time for observation in quarantine.
- The first generation progeny should be placed on a limited scale into open waters to assess ecological interactions with native species.
- All effluents from hatcheries or establishments used for quarantine purposes in recipient countries should be sterilized in an approved manner (which should include the killing of all living organisms present in the effluents).
- A continuing study should be made of the introduced species in its new environment, and progress reports submitted to ICES.

c) Section III encourages the regulatory agencies of all Member Countries to use the strongest possible measures to prevent unauthorized or unapproved introductions.

d) Section IV provides a recommended procedure for introduced or transferred species which are part of current commercial practice. Its recommendations touching on the inspection and quarantine of aquatic animals are as follows:

- Periodic inspection (including microscopic examination) of material prior to exportation to confirm freedom from introducible pests and disease agents. If inspection reveals any undesirable development, importation must be immediately discontinued. Findings and remedial actions should be reported to the ICES.

  and/or

- Quarantining, inspection and control, whenever possible and where appropriate.
- It is appreciated that countries will have different requirements toward the selection of the place of inspection and control of the consignment, either in the country of origin or in the country of receipt.

e) Section V outlines a recommended procedure for the consideration of the release of genetically modified organisms (GMOs).

The Code is written to permit broad and flexible application to a wide range of circumstances and requirements of ICES member Countries, while at the same time adhering to a set of basic scientific principles and guidelines. ICES Member Countries contemplating new introductions are requested to present to the Council a detailed prospectus of the rationale and plans for any new introduction (the contents of the prospectus are detailed in Section I of the

Code). ICES Council may then request its Working Group on Introductions and Transfers of Marine Organisms to consider the prospectus and comment on it. If necessary, the Working Group may request additional information before commenting on a proposal. If an introduction or transfer proceeds, ICES requests Member Countries to keep the Council informed about it, both by providing details of the brood stock established and the fate of the progeny, and through submitting progress reports after a species is released in the wild. The specifics of this stage are detailed in Section II of the Code.

Guidelines for Implementing the ICES Code of Practice Concerning Introductions and Transfers of Marine Species (ICES 1984).

This document (noted above to be currently under revision) specifies a number of recommended principles and practices to be followed by Member Countries when contemplating new introductions of marine species. These include:

- Notification of ICES of proposed introduction for evaluation of impacts.
- Evaluation by appropriate authorities in importing country of proposed introduction and probable effects.
- Favoured establishment of specific pathogen free broodstock in quarantine with release of progeny if healthy.
- A recommendation to always import fertile eggs and not live fish to establish broodstock populations.
- A recommendation to use approved quarantine premises, with specified operational procedures, including:
    - Treatment of all effluent from the quarantine facility.
    - Periodic and multiple laboratory and clinical inspections of imported animals, including specification of minimum sample sizes.
    - Inspection and control of individual consignments, with formal confirmation of the taxonomic status of the imported species.

The guidelines stipulate that the Code is to reduce the risk of adverse effects arising from introductions and transfers of marine species, and that it does not apply to introductions and transfers which are part of current commercial practice. They also recognize the international implications of any introductions into open waters or due to the escape of captive animals and suggest the inclusion of aquarium fishes in the guidelines.

Codes of Practice and Manual of Procedures for Consideration of Introductions and Transfers of Marine and Freshwater Organisms (Turner 1988)

This document, prepared by the ICES Working Group on Introductions and Transfers of Marine Organisms and by the EIFAC Working Party on Introductions, summarizes the "ICES 1979 Revised Code of Practice to Reduce the Risks of Adverse Effects Arising from Introduction of Non-Indigenous Marine Species" and introduces the EIFAC Code of Practice, which is directed at the reducing the risk of adverse effects arising from the introduction or transfer of inland aquatic organisms (see Turner 1988). The EIFAC Code of Practice , which is based on the ICES Code, applies essentially the same protocol to introductions and transfers of inland aquatic organisms. In relation to avoidance of possible disease transfers, it recommends the following steps:

- Examination of each proposed transfer for the possibility of introducing pathogenic organisms and parasites.
- Establishment of a brood stock in the importing country by transfer of eggs to an approved quarantine facility where they will be examined regularly for pathogens.
- If no pathogens become evident, transplant first generation progeny, but not the original import, to culture sites or the natural environment.
- Continue disease studies on these transplanted individuals.

The document includes universal protocols for (1) new introductions or transfers for commercial purposes, (2) for species used in current commercial practice, and (3) for species imported solely for scientific studies in research institutions. Within these protocols are provisions for inspection and certification, quarantine and pathological examination, and evaluation of potential ecological, environmental and genetic impacts. The document:

- Recognizes the impact of parasites and diseases arising from introductions of aquatic animals.
- Provides for the establishment of national committees or working group to ensure appropriate mechanisms for prospective applicants to import live aquatic animals and to ensure appropriate evaluation or assessment of such applications to import.
- Recognizes the need for periodic inspections of organisms for importation by importing country to confirm freedom from introduced pests and diseases.
- Recognizes the need for provision of health certification through a competent approved authority.

- Assumes, in respect to ecological problems, that escape is an inevitable consequence of introductions intended for enclosed or captive situations, and therefore, such introductions pose the same potential problems as release to the wild, with major implications for diseases and parasites.

- Accepts the principle that aquatic organisms may covertly carry pathogens without showing overt signs of clinical disease, and that they must, in most cases, be held in quarantine for life and be subject to repeated tests to establish their pathogen-free status.

- Recognizes for new introduced species, the need for the establishment and holding for life of broodstock populations in approved quarantine stations, and the release of disease and parasite-free progeny there of.

- Promotes the importation of eggs for the development of broodstock as a lower risk strategy.

- Recommends for species which are part of current commercial practice;
  - Periodic inspection by the receiving country, with discontinuation of imports if undesirable agents are found.
  - Inspection and control of each consignment on arrival.
  - Quarantine and disinfection whenever possible and where appropriate.
  - Establishment of broodstock certified free of specific pathogens.

- Recognizes that inspections to satisfy disease or other certificate requirements must be carried out by qualified personnel duly authorised by the exporting and importing countries.

- In respect to quarantine premises, emphasizes the importance of sterilization or disinfection of all equipment, effluent and wastes leaving the quarantine establishment; appropriate microbiological security entry and egress through disinfection station; limitations on visits to other aquaculture establishments; a requirement for adjacent, but physically isolated laboratory facilities; sterilization and/or disinfection of intake waters or use of water from spring, ground, artesian or well source which contains no flora or fauna; disinfection on arrival of gametes, fertilized eggs (of fish) or other stages of molluscs; prophylactic bath treatment of young fish; and accountability for all mortalities incurred in quarantine.

- Recognizes a requirement for the compilation and updating of a list of known parasites and diseases by the importing country; a certificate to be issued by the government of the country where the species originated confirming the origin of the stock, the stage to be exported and provision of a history of disease, parasites or predators.

- Notes a requirement for formal approval of quarantine premises and regular inspections by competent government specialists to ensure effectiveness, and a requirement for pathological examination in an approved laboratory by competent government specialists of specimens held in quarantine.

- Emphasizes quarantine as a minimum requirement if the exporting country cannot satisfy the health requirements of the importing country and appropriate testing in quarantine when an exporting country cannot prove it has the required capability for testing of stock.

- Notes a need for examinations of native species maintained in quarantine with the imported species to assist in the detection of disease.

- Notes wherever possible, the importation of species from a production facility or area which has been certified free of prescribed diseases over a two year period.

Appendix I of Turner (1988) gives examples of specific protocols and/or special requirements for species or species groups. The groups considered are salmonids, molluscs, and eels. Appendix II provides a review and decision model for evaluation proposed introductions of aquatic organisms, while Appendix III gives methodology s for presenting to ICES and EIFAC, proposals for introducing or transferring marine and freshwater organisms. Appendix IV give an example of a certificate of health of the origin of live fish/fish ova and an example of an exporter's declaration. Appendix V is a glossary of terms.

Overview of Current Molluscan Disease Control Measures (ICES 1991)

This document:

- Recognizes the rapidly expanding aquaculture industries based on molluscan species.

- Recognizes the difficulty in the treatment and control of disease outbreaks in molluscs in open waters.

- Clearly identifies that the optimal situation for the commercial exploitation of molluscan species is the control of spread of established diseases to new areas, and the prevention of introduction of new diseases associated with introductions and transfers of molluscs.

- Recognizes the continuing emergence of diseases of known and unknown significance.

- Recognizes the demands for transfers and introductions of indigenous and non-indigenous molluscan species.

- Reviews current disease control and quarantine legislation and requirements for a number of European Union (EU) and Non-EU countries (Belgium, Canada, Denmark, Finland, France, Germany, Iceland, Ireland, Netherlands, Norway, Portugal, Spain, Sweden, United Kingdom, United States of America).
- Notes considerable diversity in current disease control and quarantine legislation and considerable ongoing revision of such legislation with regard to prevention and control of molluscan diseases in the countries reviewed.
- Concludes that for transfers of indigenous molluscs, certification practices and procedures are of questionable value and require better definition regarding sampling regimes, numbers, and methods for disease detection; that there is a need for independent, qualified evaluation of certification programs and provision for evaluation of unrecognized pathogens; that there is a lack of agreement on disease lists of significant or insignificant diseases; and a lack of knowledge of current pathogen/parasites and a corresponding inability to define case histories of disease outbreaks.
- Concludes that for transfers or introductions of non-indigenous molluscs, problem areas exist as for transfers of indigenous molluscs, especially with respect to a need for definition of approved or acceptable certification procedures and a need for verification of significant or unrecognized diseases; that the general EIFAC/ICES protocol for introductions and transfers was compatible throughout most ICES countries, with problems relating to compatibility of disease monitoring and certification techniques and inspectors; and that the definition of quarantine and minimum specifications should be updated.

Regional Quarantine Codes, Practices and Guidelines

Outside the Asia-Pacific Region, regionally oriented guidelines are provided by the Great Lakes Fish Disease Control Committee of the Great Lakes Fishery Commission and the North American Commission of the North Atlantic Salmon Conservation Organisation, among others. European Community regulations governing the trade in living or dead aquatic animals (fish, molluscs, and crustaceans) have recently been under development. The intent of such regulations is "Establishing the animal health conditions governing placing on the market of aquaculture animals and their products" (Council of the European Communities 1991, De Kinkelin and Hedrick 1991). The EC regulations specify pathogens including infectious hematopoietic necrosis, viral hemorrhagic septicemia and seven other diseases under consideration. Provision of guidelines for fish inspections and diagnostic procedures with the aim of achieving or maintaining a certain fish health status are given, the end result of which is a certificate referring to fish from within an approved zone within EC countries, or from areas outside approved zones. Continental zones and coastal zones are defined.

Within the Asian Region, the need for quarantine and the drafting of fundamental guidelines for fish health certification programs has been the subject of a number of workshops, reports and recommendations (ADB/NACA 1991, Arthur 1987, Davy and Chouinard 1983, Davy and Graham 1979, Roberts 1981). Arthur (1995), in reviewing progress made in the Asia-Pacific Region towards establishment of quarantine systems for aquatic organisms, emphasized that quarantine programs form part of a first line of defence against possible adverse effects resulting from the introduction or transfer of exotic aquatic animals. This author notes the "Codes of Practice" for the introduction and transfer of aquatic organisms which have been developed by international organizations and stresses that such efforts must be accompanied by the development of regionally agreed-upon lists of certifiable pathogens, the standardization of diagnostics techniques and the production of health certificates of unambiguous meaning. Arthur (1995) emphasized strong commitment by national governments and the cooperation of importers/exporters as key elements in the success of these programs.

Arising from the above workshops and papers, a number of general principles and needs have been recognized and recommended for implementation:

- The establishment and implementation of a system of quarantine for aquatic animals as for other animal species.
- The establishment of central fish disease laboratory with high level diagnostic capabilities and information support.
- Establishment of quarantine controls consistent with international and regional standards.
- Specific health certification by the exporting country.
- Inspection and laboratory examination of imported fish.
- Treatment and observation of fish in quarantine.
- Safe disposal of imported water and the accompanying pests.
- Sanitary surveillance of fish farms.
- Penalties for non-compliance.

The following list summaries the recommendations related to legislation and the control of fish diseases made by scientists attending the Asian Development Bank/Network of Aquaculture Centres in Asia (ADB/NACA) Regional Study and Workshop on Fish Disease and Fish Health

Management held in Pusan, Korea in 1991. These experts agreed that countries of the region should:

- Prepare legislation to prevent the translocation of serious fish diseases both within and outside the region.
- Develop the capability of testing exports of fish to an agreed upon regional standard.
- Develop quarantine systems where imports of fish may be tested to regional standards.
- Establish a standardised system of disease testing, including a common format of health certificate.
- Compile a regional handbook of diagnostic methods.
- Quarantine and test for disease, introductions of new species in accordance with the ICES Code of Practice.
- Establish a working group of regional and international experts to deal with the above recommendations.

In the Pacific Region, the importance of quarantine in preventing spread of diseases and pests of animal and plant species has been recognised in the Pacific Islands region for many years (Morschel 1988). Quarantine for introduced fish and aquatic invertebrates has, however, been neglected, despite the social, economic and ecological importance of these species and despite their frequent introduction from other regions.

Within the Pacific Islands region, including Hawaii, more than 140 species of fish and aquatic invertebrates have been intentionally introduced or transferred over the past 200 years. These movements have been for commercial, social or ecological purposes and, with few recent exceptions, have occurred with little regard to the introduction or spread of diseases or pests. For countries in which fisheries resources and industries are of great social and economic importance, protection from diseases and pests should be a high priority of government.

General principles in the Codes and Guidelines

The OIE, ICES and EIFAC Codes contain sound general principles for the effective quarantine and certification of living aquatic animals and their products destined for introduction or translocation. A regional body to assist in evaluation of proposed introductions and translocations is strongly supported by these codes. Such a body would have a principle role in assessing proposals to introduce aquatic animals to new areas and providing expert advice on quarantine, diseases and disease control.

The ultimate need for quarantine, and the level of quarantine which is implemented, however, depends to a large extent on the individual needs of the importing countries. As such, quarantine practices and procedures for the control of diseases of concern are more appropriately developed and implemented at a national or regional level, whereby specific social, economic, industrial, and ecological considerations can be considered in relation to proposed imports, especially in regard to the relative risk of any or each proposed introduction and transfer.

Quarantine and health certification procedures should be based primarily on risk evaluation on a case by case basis, with implementation of quarantine measures appropriate to the relative risk of exotic disease incursion.

Socio-economic, Cultural and Environmental Aspects of Asian-Pacific Fisheries and Aquaculture

Social, cultural, economic and environmental factors in countries of the Asia-Pacific Region have much in common with respect to the importance of fisheries and the reliance on fisheries-based production to local economies and cultures. These factors are considerably different to those operating in Europe and North America.

Aquatic Animal Species Addressed in the Codes

For disease control and quarantine purposes, the codes primarily focus on health certification and quarantine associated with the intentional introduction or translocation of finfish, molluscs and crustaceans of economic importance as food producing animals in aquaculture. Little attempt is made to address issues arising from international movements of freshwater and marine ornamental fish, or other aquatic vertebrates or invertebrate species important in the Asia-Pacific Region.

A diverse range of aquatic animal species, including fish, molluscs, crustaceans, other invertebrates, amphibians and aquatic reptiles are present in the Asia-Pacific Region which do not naturally occur elsewhere. The major diseases affecting these species are not specifically addressed in the codes. Major industries exist in the Asia-Pacific Region based on the culture and/or capture of ornamental fish, amphibians, and to a lesser extent, aquatic reptiles. These industries are likely to expand, and require the same measures of protection from disease through an equitable system of quarantine similar to other aquatic animals and to terrestrial animal species.

ICES guidelines are concerned with marine and brackishwater animals and do not consider freshwater animals.

Diagnostic Capabilities

In order to comply with the guidelines presented in the codes, a high level of disease diagnostic capability appears necessary, in both importing and the exporting countries. Such capabilities demand specialized microbiological, histopathological and immunochemical capabilities with attendant requirements for quality control. Many countries in the Asia-Pacific Region do not have such facilities. The unequivocal adoption of the principles detailed in the OIE Code and in the OIE Diagnostic Manual for Aquatic Animal Diseases and the consequent inability to certify animals according to the OIE Code and Manual may effectively preclude exports of aquatic animals from some countries in the Asia-Pacific Region.

Pathogens, Parasites and Diseases specified in the Codes

In many cases, aquatic animals of the Asia-Pacific Region have their own particular spectrum of pathogens, parasites and diseases which are not specifically mentioned in the codes. Most of the diseases of concern listed in the codes have limited significance to tropical Asia and the Pacific, although they are relevant to Japan, China and Korea, where salmonids and other temperate species are important and farmed.

Further, there are many pathogens and parasites of aquatic animals which are ubiquitous, which are capable of inducing serious and fatal disease, especially under intensive systems of aquaculture, which are not recognized in the codes. All systems of quarantine should recognize and assess all potential causes of disease and allow for these either through testing and certification from freedom, or through effective treatment to eliminate such organisms.

A major deficiency is the absence of logical explanation regarding inclusion of diseases in the codes.

Effectiveness

Despite the existence of international codes and guidelines and health certification procedures, incursions of disease and pathogens still frequently occur.

Quarantine Zones

Where reliable veterinary administration exists, definition of disease status of specific areas or regions for certification purposes for aquatic animals (farm, country, zone) is preferred to certification of the individual species which are being moved. De Kinkelin and Hedrick (1991), however, consider that the intimate and intricate interactions between individual farms and their environments render the farm concept too small. In contrast, continents or countries may be too large, and a compromise must be reached, which may be a geographical zone, or region associated with a waterway, or catchment for quarantine purposes.

The zone concept for certification purposes is difficult when defining coastal zones for migratory fish and shellfish species and is complicated by the presence of farms within infected zones which are free of specified pathogens, especially those where the water originates from a bore or that have barriers to anadromous fish (De Kinkelin and Hedrick 1991). Issuance of a health certificate by an approved authority is accomplished only when inspections demonstrate that fish are free of specified pathogens over a suitable period, and in the absence of movements of fish onto the site during the period of observation.

General Quarantine Practices

Compliance with the above codes notwithstanding, a pragmatic approach is often adopted by importing authorities, based on health accreditation prior to imports, sometimes followed by quarantine and additional testing subsequent to importation. Certification by competent authorities for freedom from disease is an established strategy for preventing disease in introduced aquatic animals or genetic materials. This strategy is used by many countries including the USA, Canada, UK, and France, predominantly for the importation of salmonid species as eyed ova. Other strategies have been described for the importation of fish, molluscs and crustaceans.

Conclusions

- It would appear incumbent on governments of the Asia-Pacific Region to recognize the risks of uncontrolled entry of living aquatic animals and their products, and to introduce quarantine measures, especially in the face of the rapid expansion and reliance on aquaculture and other fisheries industries in the region. Protection of national fisheries resources by quarantine is far from universally accepted.

- Existing codes have been drafted to address movements of aquatic animals and their products with particular geographic regions, species, diseases and systems of aquaculture in mind. These regions, aquatic animal species, spectrum of diseases and fisheries systems differ in many ways from those found in the Asia-Pacific Region.

- Existing codes provide sound guidelines for the formulation and implementation of quarantine practices and procedures which should apply in principle to all movements of aquatic animals.

- Existing codes do not specifically address aquatic animal species other than finfish, molluscs and crustaceans. Other important aquatic animal species occur in the Asia-Pacific Region.

- Existing codes provide little flexibility in assigning a relative risk in evaluating proposed movements.
- A set of guidelines addressing the social, economic, and industrial conditions which are inherent to the Asia-Pacific Region, and which addresses specific disease problems, assesses relative risk, and does not necessarily rely on complex infrastructure and diagnostic facilities for their implementation appears warranted.
- The establishment of a regional coordinating and advisory body to collaborate with regional governments and industries on aquatic animal quarantine and fish health management issues appears urgently needed. Such a body should collaborate closely with existing international bodies (OIE, CITES) but should focus on problems and issues specific to the region.

ANNEX IX: BIBLIOGRAPHY OF SELECTED LITERATURE RELEVANT TO AQUATIC ANIMAL QUARANTINE AND HEALTH CERTIFICATION IN ASIA

ADB/NACA (1991). Fish Health Management in Asia-Pacific. Report on a Regional Study and Workshop on Fish Disease and Fish Health Management. ADB Agriculture Department Report Series No. 1. Network of Aquaculture Centres in Asia-Pacific. Bangkok, Thailand. 627p.

ADB/NACA (1996) Aquaculture Sustainability Action Plan. Regional Study and Workshop on Aquaculture Sustainability and the Environment (RETA 5534). Asian Development Bank and Network of Aquaculture Centres in Asia-Pacific. NACA, Bangkok, Thailand. 21p.

ADB/NACA (1997) Final Report on the Regional Study and Workshop on Aquaculture Sustainability and the Environment (RETA 5534). Asian Development Bank and Network of Aquaculture Centres in Asia-Pacific. NACA, Bangkok, Thailand. (In press).

Albaladejo, J.D. and Arthur, J.R. (1989). Some trichinodinids (Protozoa: Ciliophora: Peritrichida) from freshwater fishes imported into the Philippines. Asian Fisheries Science, 3:1-25.

Alimon, S.B., Vijiarungam, A.F., Ming, T.T., Yahya, M.T.B.M. and Din, M.S.B.M. (1983). Country Reports. Malaysia. p.31-34. *In* F.B. Davy and A. Chouinard (eds.) Fish Quarantine and Fish Diseases in Southeast Asia. Report of a Workshop held in Jakarta, Indonesia, 7-10 December, 1982., International Development Research Centre Canada Publication, IDRC-210e, 79p. Ottawa, Canada.

Anderson, I.G., Prior, H.C., Rodwell, B.J. and Harris, G.O. (1993). Iridovirus-like virions in imported dwarf gourami (*Colisa lalia*) with systemic amoebiasis. Australian Veterinary Journal, 70:66-67.

Andrews, J.D. (1980). A review of introductions of exotic oysters and biological planning for new introductions. Marine Fisheries Review, 42(12):1-11.

Arthur, J.R. (ed.) (1987). Fish Quarantine and Fish Diseases in South and Southeast Asia: 1986 Update. Report of the Asian Fish Health Network Workshop, Manila, 30 May 1986. Asian Fisheries Society Special Publication No. 1, 86p.

Arthur, J.R. (1995). Efforts to Prevent the International Spread of Diseases of Aquatic Organisms, with Emphasis on the Southeast Asian Region. p. 9-25. *In*: M. Shariff, J.R. Arthur and R.P. Subasinghe (eds.) Diseases in Asian Aquaculture II. Fish Health Section, Asian Fisheries Society, Manila, Philippines.

Arthur, J.R. (1996). Fish and Shellfish Quarantine - the Reality for Asia-Pacific. p. 11-28. *In*: R.P. Subasinghe, J.R. Arthur and M. Shariff (eds.) Health Management in Asian Aquaculture. FAO Fisheries Technical Paper No. 360, FAO, Rome. 142p.

Arthur, R., and M. Shariff. 1991. Towards international fish disease control in Southeast Asia. Infofish Intern. 3/91: 45-48. (republished in Bahasa Malaysia as: Arthur, R., and M. Shariff. 1991. Asia tenggara: kawalan penyakit ikan antarabangsa. Warta Akuakultur 1 (2): 30-33.)

Austin, B. and Austin, D. (1987). Bacterial Fish Pathogens. Disease in Farmed and Wild Fish. Ellis Horwood Limited, Chichester, 364p.

Bauer, O.N. (1991). Spread of parasites and diseases of aquatic organisms by acclimatisation: a short review. Journal of Fish Biology, 39:679-686.

Boustead, N.C. (1982). Fish Diseases Recorded in New Zealand, with a Discussion on Potential Sources and Certification Procedures. Fisheries Research Division Occasional Publication No. 34, Wellington, New Zealand, 29p.

Brayley, R.D. (1992). The Giant Clam: Hatchery and Nursery Manual. Australian Centre for International Agricultural Research, Canberra ACIAR Monograph No. 15, 144p.

Colorni, A., Samocha, T. and Corloni, B. (1987). Pathogenic viruses introduced into Israeli mariculture systems by imported penaeid shrimp. Bamidgeh, 39:21-28.

Copland, J.W. and Lucas, J.S. (1988). Giant Clams in Asia and the Pacific. Australian Centre for International Agricultural Research (ACIAR) Monograph No. 9, 274p.

Council of the European Communities (1991). Council directive concerning the animal health conditions governing the placing on the market of aquaculture animals and products. Official Journal of the European Communities 19.2.91:L46/1-L46/17.

Cowie, R.H. (1992). Introduced ampullariid and viviparid snails in Hawaii. Pacific Science, 46:379-398

Crawshaw, M.T. and Sweeting, R.A. (1986). *Myxobolus koi* Kudo, 1919: a new record for Britain. Journal of Fish Diseases, 9:465-467.

Cross, J.H. (ed.) (1991) Proceedings of the 33rd SEAMEO-TROPMED Regional Seminar. Emerging Problems in Food-Borne Parasitic Zoonoses: Impact on Agriculture and Public Health. Chang Mai, Thailand, 14-17 November 1990. Southeast Asian Journal of Tropical Medicine and Public Health, 22 (Supplement), 395p.

Davy, B. and Graham, M. (1979). Diseases of Fish Cultured for Food in Southeast Asia: Report of a Workshop held in Cisaura, Bogor, Indonesia, 28 November -1 December 1978. International Development Research Centre Canada Publication, IDRC-139e, Ottawa, Canada, 32p.

Davy, F.B. and Chouinard, A. (1983). Fish Quarantine and Fish Diseases in Southeast Asia. Report of a Workshop held in Jakarta, 7-10 December 1982, International Development Research Centre Canada, IDRC-210e, Ottawa, Canada, 79p.

De Kinkelin, P. and Hedrick, R.P. (1991). International veterinary guidelines for the transport of live fish or fish eggs. Annual Review of Fish Diseases, :27-40

De Kinkelin, P. (1992). The International Office of Epizootics (OIE) and its Involvement in Aquatic Animal Health Control. p. 19-37. *In*: Diseases in Asian Aquaculture I. M. Shariff, R.P. Subasinghe and J.R. Arthur (eds.) Fish Health Section, Asian Fisheries Society, Manila, Philippines.

DFO (1984). Fish Health Protection Regulations Manual of Compliance. Miscellaneous Special Publications 31 (Revised). Department of Fisheries and Oceans, Ottawa, Canada. 39p

Djajadiredja, R., Panjaitan, T.H., Rukyani, A., Sarono, A., Satyani, D. and Suprayadi, H. (1983) Country report. Indonesia . p. 19-30. *In* F.B. Davy and A. Chouinard (eds.) Fish Quarantine and Fish Diseases in Southeast Asia. Report of a Workshop held in Jakarta, Indonesia, 7-10 December, 1982, International Development Research Centre Canada, IDRC-210e, Ottawa, Canada,.79p.

Durham, P.J.K. and Anderson, C.D. (1981). Lymphocystis disease in imported tropical fish. New Zealand Veterinary Journal, 29:88-91.

Eduardo, S.L. (1991). Food-borne Parasitic Zoonoses in the Philippines, p 16-22. *In*: J.H. Cross (ed.) Proceedings of the 33rd SEAMEO-TROPMED Regional Seminar. Emerging Problems in Food-Borne Parasitic Zoonoses: Impact on Agriculture and Public Health., Chang Mai, Thailand, 14-17 November 1990. Southeast Asian Journal of Tropical Medicine and Public Health, 22 (Supplement).

Edwards, D.J. and Hine, P.M. (1974). Introduction, preliminary handling, and diseases of grass carp in New Zealand. New Zealand Journal of Marine and Freshwater Research, 8:441-454.

FAO, 1995. Code of Conduct for Responsible Fisheries. Rome, FAO. 48 p.

FAO/FIDI. (1996). The Sateate of World Aquaculture 1996. FAO, Rome. 126p.

FAO/Japan. (1995). Food, agriculture and food security: the global dimension. Information paper prepared for the 1996 World Food Summit. WFS96/TECH/1. 35 p.

Farley, C.A. (1988). Mass mortalities and infectious lethal diseases in bivalve molluscs and associations with geographic transfers of populations. Journal of Shellfish Research, 7:554.

Fryer, J.L. and Sanders, J.E. (1981). Bacterial kidney disease of salmonid fish. Annual Reviews of Microbiology, 35:273-298.

Gosting, L.H. and Gould, R.W. (1981). Thermal inactivation of infectious hematopoietic necrosis and infectious pancreatic necrosis viruses. Applied and Environmental Microbiology, 41:1081-1082.

Govan, H. (1992). Inadvertent introductions of pyramidellid parasites. Clamlines, Newsletter of the Giant Clam Research Group, No. 11:7-8. International Centre for Living Aquatic Resources Management (ICLARM), Coastal Aquaculture Network.

Gratzek, J. B., Shotts, E.B. and Blue, J.L. (1978). Ornamental fish: diseases and problems. Marine Fisheries Review, March 1978:58-60.

Gratzek, J.B., Shotts, E.B., and Blue, J.L. (1976). A survey of parasites, bacteria an viruses associated with tropical fish imported from Southeast Asia. Aquatic Mammals, 4:1-5.

Hedrick, R.P., Fryer, J.L., Chen, S.N. and Kou, G.H. (1983). Characteristics of four birnaviruses isolated from fish in Taiwan. Fish Pathology, 18:91-97.

Hoffman, G.L.(1970). Intercontinental and Transcontinental Dissemination and Transfaunation of Fish Parasites with Emphasis on Whirling Disease (*Myxosoma cerebralis*). p. 69-81. *In*: S.F. Snieszko (ed.) A Symposium on Diseases of Fish and Shellfish. American Fisheries Society Special Publication No. 5.

Humphrey, J.D. (1988). Disease Risks Associated with Translocation of Shellfish, with Special Reference to the Giant Clam *Tridacna gigas*. p. 241-244. *In*: Giant Clams in Asia and the Pacific. J.W. Copland and J.S. Lucas (eds.) Australian Centre for International Agricultural Research (ACIAR) Monograph No. 9.

Humphrey, J.D. (1995). Australian Quarantine Policies and Practices for Aquatic Animals and their Products. A Review for the Scientific Working Party on Aquatic Animal Quarantine. Bureau of Resource Sciences, Canberra. Part I: Review and Annexes, 264 p., and Part 2, Appendixes.

Humphrey, J.D. and Ashburner, L.D. (1993). Spread of the bacterial fish pathogen *Aeromonas salmonicida* after importation of infected goldfish, *Carassius auratus*, into Australia. Australian Veterinary Journal, 70:453-454.

Humphrey, J.D., Lancaster, C., Gudkovs, N. and McDonald, W. (1986). Exotic bacterial pathogens *Edwardsiella tarda* and *Edwardsiella ictaluri* from imported ornamental fish *Betta splendens* and *Puntius conchonius*, respectively: Isolation and quarantine significance. Australian Veterinary Journal, 63:369-370.

ICES (1984). Guidelines for the Implementation of the ICES Code of Practice Concerning Introductions and Transfers of Marine Species. International Council for the Exploration of the Sea, Cooperative Research Report No. 130, 20p.

ICES. 1988. Codes of Practice and Manual of Procedures for Consideration of Introductions and Transfers of Marine and Freshwater Organisms. International Council for the Exploration of the Sea, Cooperative Research Report No. 159, 44 p.

ICES (1991). Overview of Current Molluscan Disease Control Measures. ICES Working Group on Pathology and Diseases of Marine Organisms. Ostende, Belgium, February 19-22, 1991. 23p.

ICES. (1995). ICES Code of Practice on the Introductions and Transfers of Marine Organisms, 1994. International Council for the Exploration of the Sea. Pre-print, June, 1995, 5p.

JASCOFD (1987). Proceedings, Joint Advisory Subcommittee on Fish Diseases, Meeting No. 3, Brisbane, Australia, April 6, 7p.

Jiang, Y., Xu, B., Li, W., Li, Z. and Hu, Q. (1989). Isolation and identification of infectious pancreatic necrosis virus (IPNV) from imported rainbow trout (*Salmo gairdneri*) in the Peoples Republic of China. Acta Hydrobiol. Sinica., 13:353-358.

Kamiya, M. and Ooi, H.K. (1991). Current Status of Food-borne Parasitic Zoonoses in Japan. p. 48-55. *In*: J.H. Cross (ed.) Proceedings of the 33rd SEAMEO-TROPMED Regional Seminar. Emerging Problems in Food-Borne Parasitic Zoonoses: Impact on Agriculture and Public Health. Chang Mai, Thailand, 14-17 November 1990. Southeast Asian Journal of Tropical Medicine and Public Health, 22 (Supplement).

Kennedy, C.R. and Fitch, D.J. (1990) Colonisation, larval survival and epidemiology of the nematode *Anguilla crassus*, parasitic in the eel, *Anguilla anguilla*, in Britain. Journal of Fish Biology, 36:117-131.

Langdon, J.S. (1990). Disease Risks of Fish Introductions and Translocations. p 98-107. *In*: Introduced and Translocated Fishes and their Ecological Effects, A. Pollard (ed.) Australian Society for Fish Biology Workshop, Magnetic Island, 24-25 August, 1989, Bureau of Rural Resources Proceedings 8.

Lawler, A.R. and Ogle, J.T. (1977). *Dascyllus* spp.: new hosts for lymphocystis, and a list of recent hosts. Journal of Wildlife Diseases, 13:307-312.

Ledua, E. and Adams, T.J.H. (1988). Quarantine aspects of the reintroduction of *Tridacna gigas* to Fiji. p 237-240. *In*: Giant Clams in Asia and the Pacific, J.W. Copland and J.S. Lucas (eds.) Australian Centre for International Agricultural Research (ACIAR) Monograph No. 9.

Li, X. (1991). Food-borne Parasitic Zoonoses in the People's Republic of China. p. 31-35. *In*: H.J. Cross (ed.) Proceedings of the 33rd SEAMEO-TROPMED Regional Seminar. Emerging Problems in Food-Borne Parasitic Zoonoses: Impact on Agriculture and Public Health. Chang Mai, Thailand, 14-17 November 1990. Southeast Asian Journal of Tropical Medicine and Public Health, 22 (Supplement).

Lightner, D.V., Redman, R.M. and Bell, T.A. (1983). Observations on the geographic distribution, pathogenesis and morphology of the baculovirus from *Penaeus monodon* Fabricius. Aquaculture, 32:209-233.

Lightner, D.V., Redman, R.M., Bell, T.A. and Thurman, R.B. (1989). Geographic dispersion of the viruses IHHN, MBV and HPV as a consequence of transfers and introductions of penaeid shrimp to new regions for aquaculture purposes. Abstracts, Annual Meeting, National Shellfisheries Association, 12-16 February 1989, p.554.

Lilley, J.H., M.J. Philips and K. Tonguthai. 1992. A Review of Epizootic Ulcerative Syndrome (EUS) in Asia. pp. 73. Aquatic Animal Health research Institute and Network of Aquaculture Centres in Asia-Pacific, Bangkok, Thailand.

..io-Po, G.D., Pascual, J.P. and Santos, J.G. (1983). Country Reports. Philippines. p. 35-46. *In*: F.B. Davy and A. Chouinard (eds.) Fish Quarantine and Fish Diseases in Southeast Asia. Report of a Workshop held in Jakarta, Indonesia, 7-10 December, 1982, International Development Research Centre Canada, Ottawa, Canada, IDRC-210e, 79p.

..umanlan, S.C., Albaladejo, J.D. and Bondad-Reantaso, M.G. (1992). Freshwater Fishes Imported into the Philippines: Their Parasite Faunas and Role in the International Spread of Parasitic Diseases. p. 323-335. *In*: Diseases in Asian Aquaculture I. M. Shariff, R.P. Subasinghe and J.R. Arthur (eds.) Fish Health Section, Asian Fisheries Society, Manila, Philippines.

Michel, C., Faivre, B. and De Kinkelin, P. (1986). A clinical case of enteric redmouth in minnows (*Pimephales promelas*) imported into Europe as bait-fish. Bulletin of the European Association of Fish Pathologists, 6:97-99.

Morschel, J. (1988). Review of plant and animal quarantine regulations for the federated states of Micronesia. South Pacific Commission, Suva, Fiji.

NACA (1996). The 2nd Five Year Work Programme of NACA 1996-2000. Theme: Aquaculture Sustainability. Network of Aquaculture Centres in Asia-Pacific, Bangkok, Thailand, January 1996, 27p.

Natividad, J.M. (1987). Report on Philippine Fish Quarantine and Certification Programs. p. 62-72. *In*: Fish Quarantine and Fish Diseases in South and Southeast Asia: 1986 Update. J.R. Arthur (ed.). Report of the Asian Fish Health Network Workshop, Manila, 30 May 1986. Asian Fisheries Society Special Publication No. 1.

Norton, J.H., Brayley, R.D. and Anderson, I.G. (1993). A Quarantine Protocol to Prevent the Spread of Parasitic Diseases of Giant Clam (Tridacnidae) via Translocation. p. 24-26. *In*: W.K. Pitt (ed.) Biology and Mariculture of Giant Clams: A Workshop held in Conjunction with the 7th International Coral Reef Symposium 21-26 June 1992, Guam, USA. Australian Centre for International Agricultural Research (ACIAR) Proceedings No. 47.

Nui, L. and Zhao, Z. (1988). The epidemiology of IHN and IPN of rainbow trout in Northeast China. Journal of Fisheries in China 12:327-332.

NZMAF (1992). The Disease Risks Posed by Tropical Fish and New Zealand National Agricultural Security Service Standard Quarantine Procedures. New Zealand Ministry of Agriculture and Fisheries, 15p.

OIE (1995). International Aquatic Animal Health Code. Office International des Epizooties, Paris, France. 182p.

OIEFDC (1987). Transmission of Disease Agents by Fish Bait. Section 4.2., Report of OIE Fish Disease Commission, 10-11 March, 1987, Office International des Epizooties, Paris, France.

Ostland, V.E., Hicks, B.D. and Daly, J.G. (1987). Furunculosis in baitfish and its transmission to salmonids. Diseases of Aquatic Organisms, 2:163-166

Parliament of Tasmania (1933). Salmon and Freshwater Fisheries Commission: Report for Year Ending 30th June, 1933, 14p.

Pilcher, K.S. and Fryer, J.L. (1980a). The Viral Diseases of Fish: A Review through 1978. Part 1: Diseases of Proven Viral Etiology. CRC Critical Reviews in Microbiology, 7(4):287-363.

Pilcher, K.S. and Fryer, J.L. (1980b). The Viral Diseases of Fish: A Review through 1978. Part 2: Diseases in which a Viral Etiology is Suspected but Unproven. CRC Critical Reviews in Microbiology, 8(1):1-25.

Ramasoota, T. (1991). Current Status of Food-borne Parasitic Zoonoses in Thailand. p. 23-26. *In*: J.H. Cross (ed.) Proceedings of the 33rd SEAMEO-TROPMED Regional Seminar. Emerging Problems in Food-Borne Parasitic Zoonoses: Impact on Agriculture and Public Health, Chang Mai, Thailand, 14-17 November 1990. Southeast Asian Journal of Tropical Medicine and Public Health, 22 (Supplement).

Reddacliff, G.L., Hornitzky, M., Carson, J., Petersen, R. and Zelski, R. (1993). Mortalities of goldfish, *Carassius auratus* (L.), associated with *Vibrio cholerae* (non-01) infection. Journal of Fish Diseases, 16:517-520.

Roberts, R.J. (1981). Development of a Fish Quarantine System for Indonesia. Report on a visit to Indonesia on behalf of FAO, Rome. 22-10-81 - 9-11-81. Institute of Aquaculture, University of Stirling, Scotland.

Roberts, R.J., Frerichs, G.N., and Millar, S.D. (1992). Epizootic Ulcerative Syndrome - the Current Position. p. 431-436. *In*: M. Shariff, R.P. Subasinghe and J.R. Arthur (eds.) Diseases in Asian Aquaculture I. Asian Fisheries Society, Manila. Philippines.

Roberts, R.J., Macintosh, D.J., Tonguthai, K., Boonyaratpalin, S., Tayaputch, N., Phillips, M.J. and Millar, S.D. (1986). Field and Laboratory Investigations into Ulcerative Fish Disease in the Asia-Pacific Region. Food and Agriculture Organization of the United Nations, Bangkok, 214p.

Rosenthal, H. (1980). Implications of transplantations to aquaculture and ecosystems. Marine Fisheries Review, 42(5):1-14.

Sano, T. (1976). Viral diseases of cultured fishes in Japan. Fish Pathology, 10:221-226.

Sano, T., Nishimura, T., Okamoto, N., Yamazaki, T., Hanada, H. and Watanabe, Y. (1977). Studies on viral diseases of Japanese fishes. VI. Infectious hematopoietic necrosis (IHN) of salmonids in the mainland of Japan. Journal of the Tokyo University of Fisheries, 63:81-85.

SCFH (1992). Report of AHC Sub-Committee on Fish Health, Standing Committee on Agriculture, 5-6 March, Adelaide, Australia, 233p.

Shariff, M. (1980). Occurrence and treatment of ectoparasitic disease of aquarium fishes in Malaysia. Malaysian Veterinary Journal, 7:48-59

Shariff, M. and Subasinghe, R. (1992) Ornamental Fish Health: Do We Really Care? INFOFISH International 6/92:43-47.

Stewart, J.E. (1990). Introductions as factors in diseases of fish and aquatic invertebrates. Canadian Journal of Fisheries and Aquatic Sciences, 48 (Supplement 1):110-117.

Subasinghe, R.P. and Balasuriya, L.K.S.W. (1987). Fish Quarantine and Certification in Sri Lanka. p. 73-76. *In*: J.R. Arthur (ed.) Fish Quarantine and Fish Diseases in South and Southeast Asia: 1986 Update. Report of the Asian Fish Health Network Workshop, Manila, 30 May 1986. Asian Fisheries Society Special Publication No. 1.

Tong, S. and Hetrick, F.M. (1990). A study on infectious pancreatic necrosis disease of rainbow trout *Salmo gairdneri*. Journal of the Ocean University of Qingdao, 20:119-122.

Turner, G.E. (1988) Codes of Practice and Manual of Procedures for Consideration of Introductions and Transfers of Marine and Freshwater Organisms. EIFAC Occasional Paper No.23, 44p.

Wolf, K. (1966). The Fish Viruses. p. 35-101. *In*: K.M. Smith and M.A. Lauffer (eds.) Advances in Virus Research, Vol. 12. Academic Press., New York.

Wolf, K. (1988). Fish Viruses and Fish Viral Diseases. Cornell University Press. 476p.

Wong, S-Y. and Leong, T-S. (1987). Current Fish Disease Problems in Malaysia. p. 12-21. *In*: J.R. Arthur (ed.) Fish Quarantine and Fish Diseases in South and Southeast Asia: 1986 Update. Report of the Asian Fish Health Network Workshop, Manila, 30th May 1986. Asian Fisheries Society Special Publication No.1.

